2 to 22 DAYS
IN HAWAII

THE ITINERARY PLANNER
1992 Edition

ARNOLD SCHUCHTER

John Muir Publications
Santa Fe, New Mexico

John Muir Publications, P.O. Box 613, Santa Fe, NM 87504

1992 edition

Library of Congress Cataloging-in-Publication Data
Schuchter, Arnold (Arnold L.)
    2 to 22 days in Hawaii : the itinerary planner /
Arnold Schuchter.
      p. cm.
    Rev. ed. of: 22 days in Hawaii.
    Includes index.
    ISBN 1-56261-001-5
    1. Hawaii—Description and travel—1981- —Guide-
books. I. Schuchter, Arnold (Arnold L.). 22 days in
Hawaii. II. Title. III. Title: Two to twenty-two days in
Hawaii.
DU622.S35   1992
919.6904′4—dc20   91-16879
                                        CIP

Distributed to the book trade by
W. W. Norton & Company, Inc.
New York, New York

Maps   Michael Taylor
Cover map   Jim Finnell
Typography   Copygraphics, Inc.
Printer   Mc Naughton & Gunn, Inc.

CONTENTS

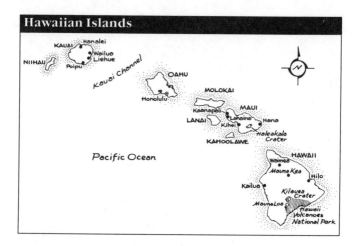

Hawaiian Islands

NIIHAU

KAUAI

Hanalei

Wailua
Liehue

Poipu

Kauai Channel

OAHU

Honolulu

MOLOKAI

Kaanapali

LANAI

Lahaina

Kihei

MAUI

Hana

KAHOOLAWE

Haleakala
Crater

Pacific Ocean

HAWAII

Waimea

Mauna Kea

Hilo

Kailua

Kilauea
Crater

Mauna Loa

Hawaii
Volcanoes
National Park

HOW TO USE THIS BOOK

A thousand years before Columbus's celebrated voyage, double-hulled canoes from Tahiti sailed to windward for thousands of miles, using ancient navigational techniques, to arrive at a legendary "heavenly homeland of the north." Near where these Polynesian mariners landed, a former sacrificial temple shares the lava and lush tropical landscape with opulent resorts and simple tents pitched on stunning white sand.

Welcome to Hawaii, where contrasting vacation pleasures, lavish and simple, manage to coexist with riddles rooted in both its Polynesian and volcanic origins. *2 to 22 Days in Hawaii* guides you, mile by marvelous mile, through 6 of the 132 islands, reefs, and shoals that make up the Hawaiian archipelago: Oahu, Maui, Molokai, Lanai, Hawaii, and Kauai.

The tour takes three weeks, but you can pick and choose among the islands to suit yourself. The itinerary works just as well for a few days or a week. The tour includes some of the most famous tourist spots, like Waikiki and Lahaina, and all of the best spots on each island, many of which most visitors never see, like the northern tip of Kohala on the Big Island and Kauai's Kalalau Trail.

Even Hawaii visitors who have "seen it all" may be pleasantly surprised by some of this book's suggestions, like the beaches east of Poipu and the scenic Kilauea Lighthouse and Bird Sanctuary tucked among the hidden beaches of Kauai's North Shore. Recently I mentioned to a well-traveled friend that my itinerary for the Big Island needed a *minimum* of eight days, with only occasional beachcombing. He expressed amazement, since he had driven around the Big Island in less than two days. Unfortunately, he also had missed most of the best sightseeing.

Take your time. Travel from one end of the chain to the other, from the youngest island to the oldest, and be utterly surprised and startled by the differences, both

obvious and subtle. Since you can fly between any two
islands for about the same low price, arrange the
sequence of islands in any way you wish.

2 to 22 Days in Hawaii starts on Oahu, where the
windward and north coasts completely contrast with
Honolulu. Oahu is rich in history and culture and as
beautiful as the other islands (although more crowded).
Don't bypass Oahu because you mistakenly equate the
whole island with Waikiki's commercialization. From
Waikiki, travel on to the windward coast and the Banzai
Pipeline. Cameras will click above and below water.

Proceed to Maui, the second-largest island and fastest-
growing tourist destination. Visit Lahaina, the splendidly
rejuvenated historic whaling town (that is growing too
fast as a shopping center). Experience Haleakala vistas
from the summit outlook and within the crater. Discover
upcountry Maui on the volcano's slopes. Travel the amazing road to blissful Hana. Relax on the beaches of
Makena.

Old Hawaii can still be found on Molokai, especially
east Molokai, together with some of the most spectacular
island scenery at Kalaupapa Peninsula, the famous leper
colony beneath 2,000-foot cliffs; the twin waterfalls of
Halawa Valley; and hidden western beaches.

On Lanai, a scenic, pine-covered mountain ridge opens
up breathtaking views of neighboring islands and then
leads to one of Hawaii's most beautiful beaches as well as
to bays adjoining historic sites. Big changes are about to
descend on Lanai, so hurry there.

The Big Island, dominated by two 13,000-foot volcanoes, invites hiking and exploring on windward and leeward coasts, including Hilo and Kailua-Kona. You can
travel from the lush Waipio Valley on the Hamakua Coast,
to Waimea grasslands or volcanic wastelands, to brilliant
orchid gardens, in a matter of minutes, dazzling your
mind and camera eye. This is an island for wide-angle and
telephoto lenses.

End the journey on Kauai, with incredibly varied cli-
mates and terrain on one small island, some of the best

beaches and hiking trails in the chain, and unforgettable
mountain and valley jungle scenery.

The 22-day tour detailed in these pages is designed for
people who want to sample the best that the Hawaiian
Islands have to offer—escaping big-resort isolation while
avoiding the regimentation of organized commercial
tours—and to spend only as much as necessary for a
wonderful vacation.

The itinerary format in this book is divided into 22
daily sections, each containing:

1. A **suggested schedule** for each day's travel and
sightseeing.

2. Detailed **transportation** and **driving** directions.

3. **Descriptive overviews** and **sightseeing highlights** (rated in order of importance: ▲▲▲ Don't miss;
▲▲ Try hard to see; and ▲ See if you get a chance).

4. **Restaurant, lodging**, and **nightlife** recommendations.

5. **Itinerary options**—excursion and adventure suggestions for travelers who have extra time.

6. User-friendly **maps** of each island, with more
detailed maps of major areas on the tour.

How Much Will It Cost?
The variety of inexpensive or moderate accommodations
and eating places can make it easy to stay within budget
in the Hawaiian Islands. Use this book to make your
choices, and your entire trip, including airfare, can average about $180 per day. For two people, the cost comes
down to about $110 per person per day including both
airfares. Excluding airfare between the mainland and
Hawaii, the 22-day budget for one person is about
$3,000, and half of that is for air and ground transporta-
tion. For the second person it's only $700 more, because
there is no extra cost for car rental and very little extra
cost for accommodations. With trans-Pacific airfare and
incidentals, one person would spend about $3,500 and
two people about $4,800. Of course, the total and per
diem average will be much lower for campers, hikers,

cyclers, and travelers determined to maintain a strict
ultra-budget itinerary.

Climate

Each island has a wet (windward) and a dry (leeward) side
of the mountains. Trade winds blow on the northeast
sides of mountains almost every day in summer, keeping
the heat and humidity down, and frequently disappear in
winter when you don't need them to moderate the temperature. When hot Kona winds take over from October
to April, the temperature is cooler on the leeward side. As
a result, notwithstanding occasional hurricanes, horren-
dous downpours, and bad Kona storms, nowhere in the
world is the temperature more constant, moderate, and
comfortable all year round.

Summer in Hawaii offers better weather than hot and
muggy mainland areas. The temperature ranges between
70 and 80 degrees Fahrenheit in summer. August and Sep-
tember, the "hottest" months, are still perfectly sunny
and beautiful. The weather is so lovely during the summer that "in season" for airfares and hotel rooms may not
mean much anymore, but there are still plenty of off-
season bargains. "High season" in Hawaii is from two
weeks before Christmas until Easter.

Getting There

Airline fares can be so confusing and changeable, from
season to season and city to city, that the only sensible
advice is to shop systematically through your travel agent
or, better yet, through several travel agents to compare
prices, since some agents tend to favor certain airlines.
Prepare your detailed itinerary for arrivals and departures
on the islands, rental cars, and either hotel or price
preferences. Start by asking for the lowest airfare, without
prepurchase requirements, *packaged with car rentals*,
for the day of the week on which you prefer to leave the
mainland.

Shop well ahead of your trip—months, if possible,
especially for winter trips—to get the lowest fares on

nonstop flights. Hawaii is the frequent fliers' favorite destination and, with triple mileage and other frequent flier club bonus programs, flights to Hawaii may be filled in almost any season. Purchase your ticket as soon as possible to guarantee the best possible discount fare. (The reservation alone doesn't guarantee the price.)

You're allowed only three free bags, including one carryon. Due to FAA pressure, airlines are strictly enforcing carryon baggage regulations. Carryons must fit under your seat or in an overhead compartment. Be sure to tag each bag with your name and hotel destination in Hawaii. Carry cosmetic essentials and a change of clothes with you, especially some beachwear, in case luggage is temporarily misrouted and delayed.

The most important fact about airline fares from mainland cities is that they are constantly fluctuating in response to competition and demand for seats. Any quotation of fares in this book or in other sources could change drastically at any time. Watch the newspapers and consult your travel agent.

At this time, from Los Angeles, Chicago, and New York, respectively, round-trip coach fares to Honolulu on United Airlines or other airlines based on midweek, 14-day advance purchase were $459, $709, and $690. Fares to Maui or Kona on United or another airline would only be $40 more round-trip.

The so-called off-season, which starts around April 1, only gives you a marginal reduction of about $20 in airfares outside of Los Angeles and New York, where you may actually pay about $20 more than "in season"! The main "off-season" advantage is that there may be more bargain seats available. Fares for children ages 2 to 12 in any season are lower: about $30 from L.A. and $150 from Chicago and New York. Children under 2 not occupying a seat travel free.

Buying just your airfare through a major packager, like MTI Vacations, could save you about $25 over United or American airlines' prices. Packagers buy seats in volume and you can benefit. If you plan to stay at first-class hotels on any or all of the islands for some or all of the nights, *look at what the packagers can offer, combining airfare, car rental, and hotels*. One of the wonderful aspects of the islands is that you can select a convenient base on any island, without driving excessively for sightseeing.

Only United and American have nonstop service from Chicago to Hawaii, but if you're willing to trade nonstop service for a lower price, Continental can get you from Chicago to Honolulu for $572 midweek, with Denver or Houston stops. Continental's fare goes up to $622 other days, but without an advance purchase requirement. You can leave midweek and come back non-midweek paying only $25 more.

Inter-Island Travel

Inter-island flights between the major islands (Oahu, Maui, Kauai, and the Big Island) are so frequent that you only have to wait a few minutes to catch the next one. For example, at last count, Aloha Airlines had 28 flights daily from Honolulu to Maui, starting at 6:00 a.m., and Hawaiian Airlines had 36. Putting the two schedules together, there's a flight every 15 minutes. There may be only 35 daily flights to choose from to Kauai, but that should do for most people. Hawaiian Airlines will get you between all of the islands, including Lanai and Molokai, flying DC-9 jets and 50-passenger Dash-7 four-engine turbo-props. On the mainland, call 800-367-5320 for reservations. Aloha flies Boeing 737s. On the mainland, call 800-367-5250.

The best news is that the maximum cost of one-way flights between islands on both airlines is still only $52.95. However, the cheaper fare on the first (5:30 a.m. or 6:30 a.m.) and last flights (6:50 p.m. or 7:55 p.m.) has risen to $46.95, which for most people removes the incentive. A book of six Aloha or Hawaiian airlines tickets costs $305.58, an increase of $60 in one year, not much of a savings compared to purchasing separate tickets. A book of six Hawaiian Airlines tickets costs $240, saving $5 per ticket or $30 for six.

Sea Link of Hawaii, Suite 230, 505 Front Street, Lahaina, HI 96761, 661-5318, recently launched the *Maui Princess* providing a $42 round-trip boat trip from Maui to Kaunakakai, Molokai. The 118-foot, four-prop craft has an air-conditioned main cabin and an open deck above. You can leave Maui at 7:30 a.m. and arrive on Molokai at 8:45 a.m. The trip can be packaged with accommodations on Molokai. This is another way to get a look at humpback whales in the channel between the two islands.

Car Rentals
Only on Oahu can the public transportation (TheBus) take you wherever you want to go in the 22-day itinerary (in fact, everywhere on the island) at the lowest fare in the hemisphere. On the Big Island, the MTA has cheap (but slow) bus service and is one of the best ways to meet locals. MTA's Hele-On Bus will take you cross-island from Hilo to Kailua-Kona, and daily buses run as far north as Waimea but not to the northern tip at Hawi, so even on Oahu, a car is almost a necessity. On Lanai, you need a four-wheel-drive vehicle to see the Munro Trail unless you plan to hike it or use a mountain bike, probably the best ways to see the island. (You won't need a four-wheel drive on any other island unless you're determined to really get off the beaten track, in which case you'll pay at least $85 per day.) On Maui and Kauai, the only alternatives to rental cars are tour buses, cruises, camper vans, helicopters, or fixed-wing planes. For rental cars, the choices on the major islands are as great as your patience. First, if at all possible, package your car rental with your airfare and accommodations. Overnighter packages from Akamai Tours (971-3131 on Oahu), Roberts Hawaii (945-2444), Island Getaways (922-4400), or Hawaiian Overnighters (922-3444) give you a round-trip fare between any two islands, a compact car (and no mileage charge), and good-to-excellent accommodations for one night for under $80 plus tax per person. Additional nights and days of car rental and accommodations are low, too,

especially for better hotels and resorts. The major airlines
(and Hawaiian Airlines on their mainland service) are
using rental cars as a bonus attraction, almost a giveaway,
to get your airfare-hotel package business. In a fly-drive
deal with an airline, which fluctuates too much these days
to accurately predict, you shouldn't have to pay more
than $22 per day or $128 per week (without insurance)
for a compact car. For quick reference, the national/
international and statewide car rental agencies' mainland
and Hawaii telephone numbers are:

   American International: mainland, 800-527-0202;
   Hawaii, 800-527-0160
   Avis: mainland, 800-331-1212; Hawaii, 800-645-6393
   Budget: mainland, 800-527-0700; Hawaii, 800-
   527-0707
   Dollar: mainland, 800-367-7006
   Hertz: mainland, 800-654-3131; Hawaii, 800-
   654-3001
   National: mainland, 800-227-7368; Hawaii, 800-
   328-6321
   Thrifty: mainland, 800-331-4200; Hawaii, 800-
   331-9191
   Holiday: mainland, 800-367-2631; Oahu, 836-1974
   Tropical: mainland, 800-367-5140; Oahu, 836-1176

The national and statewide car rental agencies will split
their car rental rates around the neighboring islands, let-
ting you rent from one company for three weeks with at
least 15 percent savings. This move eliminates bargaining
with local companies island-by-island for possibly lower
rates, but the savings are guaranteed. No matter how long
the car rental, drop it off at the same place you rented it,
on the contract date, and before the expiration time.

   Whatever car you rent, make sure it's for a flat, fixed
daily rate (or on the Big Island, a weekly rate) with unlimited mileage. In this book, listings for your arrival day on
each island provide detailed information on local,
statewide, and national car rental agencies. The tough
question becomes whether to book a car in advance with
a national or statewide agency or to wheel-and-deal

island-by-island after landing, on the chance of making a really good deal. During peak season and holiday periods, it's wise to book a car in advance, or you may be stuck without one. For the lowest rates, rent a subcompact or compact, with a stickshift and no air-conditioner (you'll rarely, if ever, need one). However, in May-October you may regret not having air-conditioning.

Accommodations
Clean, comfortable, pleasant, well-located, and moderately priced accommodations are plentiful and easy to obtain on all the Hawaiian Islands—except Lanai, where I'll show you how to avoid spending the night—if you follow this book's recommendations.

Booked in airfare-hotel packages, normally expensive condominiums can be a bargain for a group of four or more people traveling together. Your travel agent should have a plentiful supply of brochures covering these options. Certainly the major airlines do. Take your choice of package and price.

But for only one or two people to have a dream vacation in Hawaii and spend less than $60 per day on accommodations, other less expensive choices are a necessity. There are only a few motels (in Lihue on Kauai and Waimea on the Big Island), only two youth hostels (both in Honolulu), and a few cabins scattered around the state, some of them in the most superb locations like Wianapanapa State Park near Hana, Poli Poli Springs State Recreation Area in upcountry Maui, Hawaii Volcanoes National Park on the Big Island, and Kokee State Park on Kauai. With the recommended accommodations in this book, you won't go wrong.

If you arrive in Oahu or on any other island without a reservation, the best source of hotel/condo information is the Hawaii Visitor's Bureau. Their free *Membership Accommodation Guide* is the most complete and up-to-date listing, including telephone numbers and addresses in all price ranges. When you look at accommodation prices, don't forget to add 9 percent room tax. Minimum stay requirements of three days are common, especially "in season"—December 15 to April 15. Local phone calls usually are free in bed-and-breakfasts (B&Bs) and charged in hotels/condos.

Some of the very best accommodation choices are B&B houses ranging in price from $35 to $65 single or double. B&Bs are springing up on all the major islands. Check local newspapers, supermarket bulletin boards, shopkeepers, etc. But the most efficient way to find a wonderful variety of B&B bargains, hosts, and situations on all the islands is to contact: Bed & Breakfast Hawaii, Box 449, Kapaa, Kauai, HI 96746 (Kauai—822-7771, Maui—572-7692, Hawaii—959-9736); Bed and Breakfast Pacific Hawaii, 19 Kei Nani Pl., Kailua, Oahu (262-6026); Go Native Hawaii, Box 13115, Lansing, MI 48901, or 131 Puhili St., Hilo, HI 96720 (collect in Hawaii 961-2080); B and B Honolulu (595-6170); and B and B Maui Style, Box 886, Kihei, HI 96753 (800-848-5567 or 879-7865).

Camping

Hawaii offers some of the world's best camping and hiking. Hike shorelines, mountains, volcanoes, deserts, and jungle terrain, sometimes a mix in one day, and end the day at campsites that are easily accessible, near beautiful beaches, and surrounded by spectacular landscapes. Most camping is either free or costs a pittance. Some parks even offer the comfort of housekeeping cabins with all amenities which must be reserved well in advance of your trip. The climate couldn't be better for camping and hiking in 2 national parks, 16 state parks, and 36 county parks open all year. Permits and reservations are required for public camping facilities. Island-by-island, *2 to 22 Days in Hawaii* points out the best camping spots and hiking trails. The State of Hawaii offers an excellent pamphlet on camping, picnicking, hiking, overnight cabins, and group accommodations. Write: State of Hawaii, Department of Land and Natural Resources, Division of State Parks, P.O. Box 621, Honolulu, HI 96809 (808-548-7455/56). For more detailed camping and hiking information, see Robert Smith's book, *Hawaii's Best Hiking Trails.*

What and How to Pack
If you do intend to use commuter flights, it's important to know that only two normal-sized bags, weighing up to 44 pounds, are free. A third bag or baggage over 44 pounds may be carried on board on a space-available basis only. Over 80 pounds, you may have to pay extra. Not so, however, for the big carriers. On flights from the mainland, your three bags can weigh 70 pounds each as long as the height, length, and width added together doesn't exceed 62 inches. Your carryon bag should be no more than 9 inches on one side to fit under the seat.

Travel as light as possible. When in doubt, leave it home. Arrange your travel wardrobe around two colors that allow you to mix and match tops and bottoms (pants, skirts, and shorts) for lots of variety with the fewest possible items. Plan to do laundry at least once and possibly twice a week to recycle your clothing. Pack jeans, shorts, loose-fitting shirts, and dresses (aloha shirts and muumuus await your shopping in Waikiki). Pack wrinkle-free and colorful clothing, dress shoes, walking and jogging shoes, and sandals. Hawaiians dress very casually, but bring one moderately dressy outfit for the rare nightlife or dining places that require it, if that's in your plan. Don't forget one very warm outfit, and strong but comfortable walking or hiking shoes for the trip up to Haleakala on Maui or Mauna Kea, Mauna Loa, and Volcanoes National Park on the Big Island. Pack a sweater or jacket for cool days or evenings and trips in the mountains, a poncho for windward Hawaii and other windward island destinations, and a small, flat, empty bag for beach trips and shopping. Pack your cosmetics, shampoo, and other liquids in plastic bottles and place them in reclosable plastic bags to prevent leakage in unpressurized airplane baggage compartments. Take sunblock tanning lotion, your favorite moisturizer, a hat if you're sensitive to sun, sunglasses, and a bathing suit.

Recommended Reading
There are a few books that you might consider taking
with you to supplement *2 to 22 Days in Hawaii*. For
hikers, *Hawaii's Best Hiking Trails* by Robert Smith (Ber-
keley, Calif.: Wilderness Press, 1985) is indispensable.
This is a readable, well-organized guide, with everything
you need to know about preparing for Hawaii's hiking
trails. Smith tells you how to get to the trailhead (bless-
ings on the author). Each hike is rated, described realisti-
cally, with a clearly drawn trail map showing sufficient
detail, key trail features and sights, complete camping
information, where to picnic or take a break, flora and
fauna you'll find in each area, and tidbits of background,
description, and explanation that make hiking more
enjoyable. Craig Chisholm's *Hawaiian Hiking Trails* (Lake
Oswego, Oreg.: The Fernglen Press, 1986) is also an excellent guidebook. Both are very scarce in U.S. bookstores.
    S. H. Sohmer, Chairman of the Department of Botany,
Bishop Museum, and his coauthor and photographer,
Robert Gustafson, have created an extremely informative
and attractive guide, *Plants and Flowers of Hawaii* (Honolulu: University of Hawaii Press, 1987). Lavishly illustrated with over 150 beautiful color photographs of
Hawaii's native plants, the book is compact enough to
carry with you, and its photographs will enable you to
identify the different habitats and plant life you'll see on
each island. For divers, snorkelers, and all those who
want to understand Hawaii's underwater environment,
An Underwater Guide to Hawaii by Ann Fielding and Ed
Robinson (Honolulu: University of Hawaii Press, 1987)
describes the geologic formation of the islands and coral
reef building and provides over 200 color photographs of
marine life. Both books are difficult to find except in
specialized travel bookstores.
    Hawaii Handbook by J. D. Bisignani (Chico, Calif.:
Moon Publications, 1990) contains several pounds of
valuable background and travel information and budget-
oriented eating and accommodations recommendations,
with plentiful photos, excellent illustrations by Diana

Harper, and plenty of maps (many of them difficult to read without a magnifying glass).

Peter Bellwood's *The Polynesians: Prehistory of an Island People* (New York: Thames and Hudson, 1987) provides background on the Polynesians and their culture, religion, arts, and crafts.

The Bishop Museum has published numerous volumes on pre-European Hawaiian culture. One of the best, written in the nineteenth century, is *Hawaiian Antiquities* by David Malo (Bishop Museum Press, 1971).

Gavan Daws's *Shoal of Time* (Honolulu: University of Hawaii Press, 1974) is a comprehensive history, and *Hawaii Pono* by Lawrence H. Fuchs (Harcourt Brace Jovanovich, 1961) shows you twentieth-century Hawaii as viewed by a sociologist. James Michener's very long historical novel, *Hawaii* (Bantam Books), is a combination of fact and fiction covering the entirety of Hawaii's history, not to be taken too literally.

If you need any further encouragement to make reservations and purchase tickets to Hawaii, Jeff Gnass's *Hawaii, Magnificent Wilderness* (Englewood, Colo.: Westcliffe Publishers) will clinch the decision. In panoramic views and close-ups, the book captures many of the most superb landscapes and contrasts in Hawaii. Robert Wenkam has produced four beautiful pictorial books: *Honolulu Is an Island* (1978), *Maui: The Last Hawaiian Place* (1980), *Hawaii's Garden Isle: Kauai* (1979), and *The Big Island Hawaii* (1975), all Chicago: Rand McNally.

Whaling ships, refitting in Lahaina for the next season of hunting in Pacific and Hawaiian waters, brought "civilization," commerce, and missionaries to Hawaii, along with the rapid destruction of the local population. The beautiful *Whalesong: A Pictorial History of Whaling in Hawaii* by MacKinnon Simpson and Robert B. Goodman (Honolulu: Beyond Words Publishing Co.) is a superbly illustrated and reproduced retrospective. All of the profits from this labor of love go to the Whalesong Fund for whale research. The dozen or so species of whales and many kinds of dolphins you might see will be easy to identify with *The Whales of Hawaii* (produced by Stanley M. Minasian, written by Kenneth C. Balcomb II, illustrated by Larry Foster, published by the Marine Mammal Fund, available from Hawaiian Resources Co. Ltd., 1123 Kapahulu Ave., Honolulu, HI 96816) in hand.

For Hawaiian trivia, read *Incredible Hawaii* by anthropologist Terence Barrow and illustrator Ray Lanterman (Rutland, Vt., and Tokyo: Charles E. Tuttle Company). Factual and interesting anecdotes cover history, culture, and superstition on each island.

My *Shopper's Guide to Arts and Crafts in the Hawaiian Islands* (Santa Fe, N.M.: John Muir Publications, 1990) tells all about the artists working on each island. It also includes additional suggestions for sightseeing, accommodations, and dining.

The University of Hawaii Press has produced full-color topographic maps for only $2.50 for each island. These detailed maps show every town, point of interest, type of road and trail, stream and waterfall, ridge and peak, and beach and park.

For More Information

For informative brochures on all facets of life and sightseeing on the islands, visit or contact Hawaii Visitor's Bureau offices on the mainland or in Hawaii. On the mainland: **Chicago**, 180 N. Michigan Avenue, Suite 1031, Chicago, IL 60601, 312-236-0632; **Los Angeles**, Central Plaza, 3440 Wilshire Boulevard, Room 502, Los Angeles, CA 90010, 213-385-5301; **New York**, 441 Lexington Avenue, Room 1407, New York, NY 10017, 212-986-9203; **San Francisco**, 50 California Street, Suite 450, San Francisco, CA 94111, 418-392-8173. In Hawaii: **Oahu**, Waikiki Business Plaza, 2270 Kalakaua Avenue, Suite 801, Honolulu, HI 96815, 923-1811; **Maui**, 25 N. Puunene Avenue, Kahului, HI 96732, 244-9141; **Hawaii**, Hilo Plaza, 180 Kinoole Street, Suite 104, Hilo, HI 96720, 961-5797, and 75-5719 W. Ali Drive, Kailua-Kona, HI 96740, 329-7787.

DAY 1 Fly from the U.S. mainland to Honolulu, Oahu, a 5½ -hour flight from the West Coast. Hawaii is two to five hours earlier than back home. Rent a car at the airport for the next three days unless you've decided to use TheBus, the best public transportation bargain in the United States. Waikiki has plenty of inexpensive and comfortable places to stay and eating places to match, especially for ethnic food lovers. Absorb the sunshine on a Waikiki beach or visit the marine wonders of Sea Life park. Drive up to Diamond Head's crater for a superb panoramic view of Oahu's south coast. End the afternoon on Diamond Head or Koko Head and return to Waikiki for dinner and nightlife, or sensibly retire for an early bedtime.

DAY 2 An ancient Hawaiian sacrificial site in the Punchbowl Crater today is the National Memorial Cemetery of the Pacific and the profoundly contrasting start of a joyful trip over the Pali Highway to windward Oahu. Head up Nuuanu Valley, with grand estates, rich Hawaiian history, and the vivid spectrum of Hawaiian royal life and death: the Royal Mausoleum, and Hanaiakamalama, better known as Queen Emma's Summer Palace. On the windward coast, visit exquisitely landscaped Japanese enclaves, the Haiku Gardens and Valley of the Temples, with its Byodo-In Temple resting serenely under the Koolau Cliffs, and the Polynesian Cultural Center. Visit your choice of the best-kept secrets of the windward coast, the fine beaches of Kualoa County Park, Malaekahana Bay, and Goat Island. Return to your accommodations or consider staying on the windward coast to continue on to the North Shore tomorrow.

DAY 3 The North Shore in winter responds violently to distant stormy Arctic wave pulses, transforming the otherwise placid coast into thunderous surf-pounding

offshore reefs at Sunset Point, Banzai Pipeline, and Waimea Bay. From Puu O Mahuka Heiau, survey Waimea Bay,
calm in spring, summer, or fall. Visit the beautiful and
informative Arboretum in Waimea Falls Park and have
lunch in the park. Move on to delightful Haleiwa for Matsumoto Grocery's renowned shave-ice dessert. Return to
downtown Honolulu through the pineapple fields of
Wahiawa Plains, past Schofield Barracks (remember the
movie *From Here to Eternity*?) and Pearl Harbor, with an
optional stop at the USS *Arizona* Memorial. Before leaving Oahu, visit the Bishop Museum, the world's foremost
collection of Pacific and Polynesian artifacts, art, and
research. Then take a walking tour of Honolulu's historic
attractions of 100 years ago: Iolani Palace, Washington
Place, several churches, the Mission Houses Museum, and
the Hawaii Maritime Center. Your stroll through Old
Honolulu ends in Merchant Street and Chinatown and
includes a superb Chinese dinner.

DAY 4 Check out very early this morning for the flight to
Kahului Airport, Maui. Rent a car at the airport and drive
to the historic waterfront town of Lahaina, a fascinating
and charming walking town and the ideal base for touring
west Maui's coastline. After lunch, drive up the west coast
and savor superb Kapalua Beach. After dinner in Lahaina,
it's very early to bed for anyone planning to catch the
sunrise on Haleakala's summit.

DAY 5 Try to rise at 3 a.m. to see an unforgettable sunrise
from Haleakala volcano. (Or start out later in the morning
and stay on the mountain for an awesome sunset.) Drive
to the Puu Ulaula Visitor's Center at Haleakala's summit
and then hike on Halemauu or Sliding Sands Trail. Afterward, tour one of the most beautiful, interesting, and
overlooked parts of Hawaii—the upcountry. Check out
the distinctive character and shopping in Makawao and
Paia. Tour the Kula Botanical Gardens, local protea nurseries, and end the afternoon wine-tasting at the Tedeschi
Winery.

DAY 6 Leave early for Hana Town. The incomparable
(and much maligned) Hana Highway twists in and out of
hundreds of switchbacks, with waterfalls in almost every
gulch, dozens of narrow bridges, and bordering cliffs that
drop off to pounding surf. Stop along the way at Twin
Falls, Huelo, Waikamoi Ridge, Kaumahina State Wayside,
Wailua and Wailua Lookout, Puaa Kaa State Park, and
Waianapanapa State Park. Swim at Hamoa Beach and visit
beautiful Helani Gardens. Have lunch and tour Hana and
its outskirts. Decide whether to spend the next few hours
on a scenic tour to Ohe'o Gulch, enjoy marvelous horseback riding on the Hana-Kaupo Coast, or just ease into
relaxed Hana sightseeing. Stay in Hana overnight.

DAY 7 On the drive back from Hana, stop off at the
Keanae Arboretum. Drive to Kihei on the southwest coast
by way of Paia and the upcountry, with a stop for lunch.
Your destination today is sun and surf at beautiful Makena
Beach past Wailea resort and the Maui Prince resort, with
an option of driving even farther to La Perouse Bay for
sightseeing or snorkeling. Your relaxation is cut short by
the afternoon flight to Molokai. Allow time to drop off
your rental car at the Kahului Airport before the flight to
Molokai's Hoolehua airstrip.

DAY 8 Spend the morning on an unforgettable mule ride
(or walk down) to Kalaupapa, the former leper colony on
land- and sea-locked Makanalua Peninsula. After a picnic
lunch and tour of this historic peninsula, return to
Kualapuu and drive to Palaau State Park and (as an option)
then to Waikolu Overlook for spectacular views of the
valleys and pali below. Consider a tour of the Kamakou
Preserve to see hundreds of species of Hawaiian flora.
Stay overnight near Kaunakakai.

DAY 9 The drive along the south shore to Halawa Valley
at the eastern end of Molokai is as much a part of today's
tour as the valley itself. Stop at ancient fishponds and
temple ruins, churches and other historic sites, and lovely

small shady beaches inviting swims and relaxation. The hike to Moaula Falls in Halawa Valley is over two hours round-trip. Follow directions carefully to the falls. Then drive to the western end of the island, through Molokai Ranch, to tour Molokai Ranch Wildlife Park and explore beautiful Papohaku Beach, Molokai's prettiest beach.

DAY 10 Rise early to spend one very full day on nearby Lanai. After flying to Lanai, pick up your four-wheel drive, picnic supplies, a detailed trail map, and information on road conditions, and head for the Munro Trail. Drive up to The Hale, highest point on the island, for great views of the Hawaiian Islands. Drive down to Manele Road, leading to beautiful Manele and Hulopoe bays. Swim and/or snorkel at Hulopoe Bay. In the village of Kaunolu on the southwestern tip of Lanai are the remains of an important temple, Kamehameha's summer house, and other historical and legendary sites. Return to Molokai for the night.

DAY 11 Leave early for Hilo on the Big Island. Welcome to a profusion of blossom colors on the "Orchid Island," and the black lava and steaming fissures of the "Volcano Island." A counterclockwise exploration of these fascinating contrasts starts in Hilo, whose 1940s appearance and pace make the transition from quiet Molokai and Lanai much easier. Visit the Lyman Mission House and Museum and then drive south a few miles to a local nursery with one of the largest collections of orchids in the state. On a stroll through Hilo's historic downtown, you'll discover many old and beautiful wooden buildings with overhanging awnings to shelter you from possible rain. If this is a winter trip, prepare to be drenched occasionally by the same rain that makes Hilo a greenhouse of exotic tropical flowers.

DAY 12 After visiting an early morning fish auction and another spectacular botanical garden, go back in time to the sugar plantation world of prewar Hawaii on the

Hamakua Coast north of Hilo. Drive along Mamalahoa
Highway, the old road bypassed by main Highway 19.
Start by following the four-mile scenic drive past Onomea
Bay. Cross many one-lane wooden bridges in a gently
rolling plateau covered with sugarcane fields ending at
cliffs over the sea. After taking a spur road to beautiful
Akaka and Kahuna falls, head for the town of Honokaa.
You'll pass jungle canyons, each with hidden waterfalls
cascading from lush steep slopes, and a handful of tiny
plantation towns. A few miles north of Honokaa, home of
the Hawaiian Holiday Macadamia Nut Factory, lies one of
the great adventures of the Hawaiian Islands, exploring
Waipio Valley.

DAY 13 This morning explore Waimea and the town of
Kamuela, the domain of one of the world's largest
ranches, the 225,000-acre Parker Ranch. The Parker family history is displayed in a museum that's worth visiting
before you follow the Kohala Mountains to the remote
northern tip of the Big Island. Leaving Waimea for north
Kohala on Highway 250, once again you go back in time,
this time to the plantation towns of Hawi and Kapaau. At
the Pololu Valley Lookout, be adventurous and walk
down to the black sand beach. As an option, drive off the
beaten track to find Kamehameha's birthplace, the
ancient sacrificial temple Mookini Luakini Heiau, and the
reconstruction of a 600-year-old fishing village.

DAY 14 From luxuriant forests and grassy upcountry
rangeland, drive down to the hot and very dry lava shores
of south Kohala. From a vision of Laurence Rockefeller,
the Mauna Kea Beach Hotel grew out of this inhospitable
coast filled with ancient temples, legends, and prophe-
cies. The hotel's halls and public areas are filled with
Asian and Pacific art and artifacts. After lunch, see some
of the finest Hawaiian rock carvings at Puako and petroglyphs along the King's Highway footpath. Drive to a
string of other resorts and gorgeous bays with perfect
crescents of golden coral sand beaches (Anaehoomalu,

Kaun'oa, and Hapuna), bordered by palms and delicate
vegetation.

DAY 15 The sun-soaked region of jagged lava fields and
tropical waters around the Kona Coast's major resort
town, Kailua-Kona, still offers some of the same attractions that drew Hawaii's royal families here in another
era. Links with this historic Hawaiian life-style can be
seen at the restoration of King Kamehameha's Royal Palace grounds; at Hulihee Palace, the summer residence of
Hawaiian kings; and at displays in the Hotel King Kamehameha. In the afternoon, drive through hillsides thick
with coffee trees producing famous Kona beans, to the
Kealakekua Bay area and the white obelisk marking the
spot where Captain Cook met his untimely death. Nearby
is one of Hawaii's most fascinating historic sites, the Pu'u-
honua O Honaunau National Historical Park, where
priests in ancient Hawaii pardoned kapu (taboo) breakers.
Return to Kailua-Kona for sunset, dinner, and local
nightlife.

DAY 16 Drive south along Route 11—stopping at the old
fishing village of Milolii—to the barren lava of Kau, to
South Point, where Polynesian voyagers made their first
landfall. After a side trip to the southernmost point in the
United States, and then Punaluu's black sand beach, you
arrive at Hawaii Volcanoes National Park. Explore trails
from Crater Rim Road. Have dinner and stay overnight at
Kilauea Lodge.

DAY 17 Return to the Visitor's Center to see a film on
Hawaii's volcanic history and to get up-to-date informa-
tion on today's trails and roads. Drive up Mauna Loa Strip
Road to Bird Park for a walk through a densely forested
bird sanctuary and a picnic lunch. Continue up the Strip
Road to the overlook at the trailhead. Descend to the Kau
Desert Footprints Trail. Afterward, at the Volcano Art
Center, browse through an excellent collection of authen-
tic Hawaiian arts and crafts housed in the original Volcano
House.

DAY 18 From the Crater Rim Road, follow the Chain of Craters Road to the Pu'u Loa Petroglyphs and the Wahaula Heiau, one of the island's first temples. Return to Crater Rim Road and Highway 11 to Keaau, and Highway 130 to the Puna Coast. Stop in the picturesque town of Pahoa for lunch and a stroll. Follow Route 137 to Kumukahi Lighthouse at Kapoho Point, where a huge lava flow miraculously parted around the lighthouse and closed again at the sea. On Route 132, head to Pahoa through thousands of acres of lava flow to lush Lava Tree State Park, where lava hardened around the skeletons of a fossilized ohia forest. From here it is only 30 minutes to Lyman Field Airport for the flight to Lihue Airport on Kauai.

DAY 19 On the way to an early trip up Waimea Canyon, stop at the beautiful Ka'lmi Na'auao Hawaii Nei, Hanapepe Canyon Lookout, and Waimea, Captain Cook's first landing place on Kauai. Lunch at the Kokee Lodge Restaurant, in Kokee State Park, or picnic in the adjoining meadow. Continue up to breathtaking Kalalau Lookout, overlooking the Na Pali Cliffs to the blue ocean thousands of feet below. Drive to accommodations, dinner, and nightlife in the Poipu beach area.

DAY 20 Eat breakfast in Koloa Town, the state's first sugar plantation, refurbished as a shopping area. Pick up a picnic lunch in Koloa and return to Poipu to drive or walk to off-the-beaten-track beaches like Shipwreck and Mahaulepu for beachcombing, swimming, and lunch. Tour in and around Poipu to see the Spouting Horn blowhole and beautiful Kiahuna Gardens. Browse or shop, especially for the wares of jewelry vendors around Spouting Horn.

DAY 21 Some of the state's most beautiful and hidden beaches are found along the North Shore drive to Hanalei Valley, only 50 miles from Poipu. Stop at some of these beaches: Kealia, Anahola, Moloaa, Larson's, Secret, Kalihiwai, and Anini. Pass Hanalei, Lumahai, and Haena

beaches and ten single-lane bridges on the way to your
picnic destination at the end of the road, Kee Beach.
Spend the evening in Hanalei.

DAY 22 Visit Wailua River State Park, the former home of
Hawaii's royalty, midway along the east coast, or visit
Grove Farm Homestead. Lunch at the Kilohana Plantation, a beautifully landscaped historic site and museum,
with a distinctive group of art and craft shops covering
Hawaii, the Pacific, and Asia. If it's December through
March, this may be your last chance on this trip to whale-
watch, which is an option from Lihue's waterfront. After
three of the best vacation weeks of your life, it's time to
return to the U.S. mainland with an enviable collection of
photos and stories.

OAHU: HONOLULU AND
WAIKIKI/DIAMOND HEAD

After checking in at your accommodations, get some of
Hawaii's wonderful sunshine and fresh air on the Diamond
Head end of Waikiki. Pick up a plate lunch take-out for a
picnic, cool off in the calm Waikiki waters, and then head
for Diamond Head to get a great view of eastern Honolulu and Waikiki. Visit Sea Life Park and find the right
spot for sunset viewing.

Suggested Schedule

8:00 a.m.	Fly from U.S. mainland to Honolulu, Oahu.
12:00 noon	Arrive in Honolulu, and take a bus, limo, or rental car to your Waikiki accommodations.
1:00 p.m.	Snack lunch at Kapiolani Beach Park.
2:00 p.m.	Swim at Kuhio Beach Park or anywhere at the Diamond Head end of Waikiki, or drive to Diamond Head and climb to the summit.
3:30 p.m.	Head for Sea Life Park.
Sunset	Diamond Head or Koko Head.
7:00 p.m.	Return to accommodations for cleanup before dinner.
8:00 p.m.	Dinner in the Waikiki area.
10:00 p.m.	Enjoy some of Waikiki's nightlife (but at least think about early to bed to ease jet lag).

Flying from the U.S. Mainland to Oahu
Most flights land at Honolulu International Airport. The
flying time to Honolulu from Los Angeles is 5½ to 6
hours. From Chicago, it's a 9-hour nonstop flight. One-
stop from New York is about 11 hours in the air and a
13-hour trip. Return flights are slightly shorter.

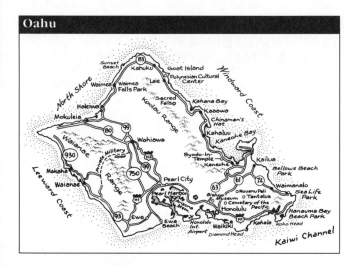

Getting Around Oahu

From the Airport: Many hotels have courtesy pickup, and their phones are near the baggage area. A taxi from the airport to Waikiki costs about $20 with tip depending on the distance and the number of bags. Call SIDA taxis (836-0011) for the Honolulu area or Aloha State Taxi (847-3566) for elsewhere on the island. Better, use the Gray Line Airporter (834-1033) to Waikiki, Airport Motorcoach (926-4747), or Waikiki Airport Express, all $5 per adult. Unfortunately, on the unbeatable TheBus, only a small carryon bag (not a backpack) that you can hold in your lap is allowed. Buses #8 and #20 pass just outside the airport and can take you to Ala Moana Terminal to pick up connecting buses.

   TheBus: No matter where you go on Oahu, for a continuous trip in the same direction, TheBus costs only 60 cents (exact change only), free if you're under 6 or over 65. Transfers are free for a bus on a different line in the same direction, so you can get on and off free following this rule. You can do a complete circuit of the island, windward and leeward coasts, in about 4 hours on bus #52. Look for the bus painted yellow, brown, and orange, which has its main terminal at the Ala Moana Shopping Center on the Kona Street side of the ground-floor parking lot. At the information booth there, you can pick up maps and schedules, or call 942-3702.

These are TheBuses to some of the primary destinations from the Ala Moana Terminal:

Airport: #8 and #20

Waikiki Beach: #2, #4, #8, #14, and #20

Arizona Memorial/Pearl Harbor: #20, #50, #51, and #52

Wahiawa, Honolulu downtown, and Chinatown: #1 through #9, #11, and #12

Hanauma Bay: #1 and #57

Sea Life Park: #57

Polynesian Cultural Center: #52

Queen Emma Palace: #4

Driving: Avoid driving during rush hours (7 to 9 a.m. and 4 to 6 p.m.) anywhere near Honolulu or the Pali roads. Buy a copy ($6.25) of *Bryan's Sectional Maps, Oahu*, which is indispensable for finding towns, subdivisions, parks and recreation areas, shopping centers, and all attractions.

Car Rentals: Car rental prices may amaze you. For example, a Hertz subcompact (or even a compact if you are very nice) can be rented for $88 per week minus any discounts such as AAA's 5 percent for members. If at all possible on Oahu, rent a car—you'll need it. The expensive part of car rental is the insurance, so leave home with adequate coverage to save $9 + per day in Hawaii. Avis, 836-5531; Budget, 836-1700; Dollar Rent-A-Car, 926-4251; and Hertz, 836-2511, are all at the airport. National, 836-2655, is outside the airport. A phone call away, smaller firms offer slightly better deals. For older cars at bargain rates, call AAA Rents, 524-8060, or Alpert's Used Cars, 955-4370. Other small local firms include Aloha Funway Rentals, 834-1016; Compact Rent-A-Car, 833-0059; Five-O Rent-A-Car, 836-1028; Holiday, 836-1974; Thrifty, 836-2388; Travelers Rent-A-Car, 833-3355; Tropical, 836-1041; and VIP Car Rental, 946-1671.

Bikes and Mopeds: Most sightseeing in the Honolulu area is within easy reach of bicycles or mopeds. The main problem with biking on Oahu is heavy traffic on the coastal roads. Rent a mountain bike to get off the main roads. Bikes at Aloha Funway Rentals are $10 per day. Mopeds at Funway are $14 for 24 hours. For more cycling information, contact Hawaii Bicycling League, Honolulu. Guided bicycle tours of Oahu and other islands are available through Island Bicycle Adventures, 569 Kapahulu Avenue, Honolulu, HI 96815, 732-7227, at costs of $90 to $120 per day including food and lodging.

Sightseeing Highlights
Kapiolani Beach Park—Named after King Kalakaua's wife, Queen Kapiolani, this park near the east end of Waikiki includes the world's largest saltwater swimming pool (War Memorial Natatorium), the **Aquarium** (923-9741, $2.50 donation per adult), the **Honolulu Zoo** (971-7171, 8:30 a.m to 4 p.m. daily, adults $3, children 12 and under free), and a rose garden at Monsarrat and Paki avenues. **Artists of Oahu/Sunday Exhibits,** along the fence at the Honolulu Zoo, bring together a large number of the island's professional and part-time artists and craftspeople on Wednesdays and weekends between 10 a.m. and 4 p.m.

▲▲▲Diamond Head—This extinct volcano rising 760 feet above the east end of Waikiki can be reached by car from Monsarrat Avenue; then you can hike a half hour to the top. The crater got its name from British sailors in the early 1800s who found calcite crystals on the slopes and thought they were diamonds. Head to Kapiolani Park, then take Diamond Head Road and climb the kiawe-covered Kuilei Cliffs to the cliffside lighthouse. Beneath the cliffs are two parks you can walk down to: **Diamond Head Beach Park** and **Kuilei Cliffs Beach Park,** which has three turnouts—stop at the second one.

Diamond Head Road descends between cliffside houses to Kahala Avenue and then climbs to the crater's east side. Pass through Fort Ruger (no longer operative)

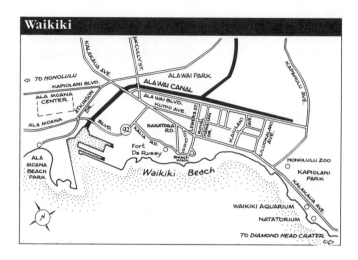

and down the crater's western slope on Monsarrat Avenue. At Diamond Head Road and 18th Street, take a left at a sign marked "Civ-Alert USPFO" and drive right into Diamond Head through a tunnel where the huge crater opens up to nothing more than the Hawaii National Guard Armory, the FAA's flight traffic control center, and many kiawe trees descended from a single seed planted by a priest 160 years ago. Your goal is the panoramic view from the crater's rim, reached by a 0.7-mile trail (one way) up the northwest side of the crater. There are many lookout points along the way, as well as tunnels and bunkers, former gun emplacements, and towers. The observation point at the summit is an outstanding picnic spot.

▲▲ **Koko Head and Koko Crater**—Travel along tree-shaded Kahala Avenue, past the Kahala Hilton to Kealaolu Avenue, then back to Kalanianaole Highway, through Henry J. Kaiser's 6,000-acre Hawaii Kai development to Koko Head Regional Park, scenic lookouts, and Koko Head Crater at 1,200 feet. On the crest of Koko Head is a side road that leads to a parking lot above picturesque Hanauma Bay, a volcanic crater opened to the ocean. Paths wind down the steep hillside to the coconut palm-fringed bay with tidepools, rocky headlands, and a pretty

white sand beach. From one side of the lookout above
Halona Blowhole, geysers shoot through the submerged
lava tube. Halona Cove and Sandy Beach Park are especially nice places to have picnics.

▲▲ **Sea Life Park**—Opposite **Makapuu Beach Park,**
this park is worth visiting if only to see the 300,000-
gallon Hawaiian Reef Tank, a three-story glass tank containing thousands of species of marine life. Also be sure to
see the Ocean Science Theater's trained dolphins, sea
lions, and penguins. It's open from 9:30 a.m. to 5 p.m. (10
p.m. on Thursday, Friday, and Sunday), adults $12.50, 7-
to 12-year-olds $8.50, 4- to 6-year-olds $4.50. The
Pacific Whaling Museum (free) just outside the entrance
displays an outstanding collection of whaling artifacts.
Rising above the coastal highway are the 1,200-foot
Makapuu Cliffs. Sea Life Park is at the base of these cliffs.
The Kalanianaole Highway brings you through Waimanalo, past Waimanalo Beach, the longest stretch of
sand on Oahu (site of the Robin Masters estate and the
home of *Magnum P.I.*), to the junction of Highway 61,
where you turn left onto the Pali Highway.

Where to Stay

Through one telephone call to the **Outrigger Hotels
Hawaii** (800-367-5170), you can discuss a wide range of
prices and rooms as close to the beach at budget prices as
you can find in Waikiki. **Outrigger Coral Seas Hotel**,
250 Lewers Street, 923-3881, has appealing rooms, is
decently decorated, with lanais, and is a stone's throw
from the beach. Ask for a kitchenette. Off-season, rooms
without kitchenettes are $50 to $75 and with kitchenettes
$65 to $85 ($10 more in season). **Outrigger Waikiki
Surf**, 2200 Kuhio Avenue, 922-5777 or 800-733-7777,
has renovated standard units without kitchenettes for $45
to $60 and with kitchenettes for $60 to $70 off-season,
$15 more during peak season. The newly refurbished
Outrigger Waikiki Surf East, 420 Royal Hawaiian Avenue, 923-7671 or 800-733-7777, has single and double
rooms for $45 to $55, $5 more in peak season. Likewise,

the **Outrigger Waikiki Surf West**, 412 Lewers Street, 923-7671 or 800-733-7777.

If you can't find what you're looking for through Outrigger Hotels, contact **Aston Hotels and Resorts** (1-800-922-7866) and ask especially about the completely remodeled **Hawaiian Monarch**, 444 Niu Street, 949-3911, with rooms from $59 to $70 off-season without kitchenettes.

Look on Beachwalk, the quiet little street that runs from Kalakaua down to the beach, for more of the best accommodation bargains in Waikiki. You can get a small one-bedroom apartment for $45 to $60, without tub or free local calls but right near the beach, at the **Niihau Apartment Hotel**, 247 Beachwalk, 922-1607. **Hawaiiana Hotel**, 260 Beachwalk, 923-3811 (800-367-5122), has 95 very simply furnished garden units with kitchens, situated around a beautiful tropical garden and two swimming pools. Complimentary breakfast, free parking, and washer/dryer are part of the $75 to $85 single, $80 to $90 double rates during the summer season (Apr. 20 to Dec. 17). Winter rates are only $5 higher. Free parking in the rear of the hotel is a plus.

My favorite B&B belongs to charming Paula Luv, folk dancer, instructor, and Pacific region traveler. Atop Wilhelmina Rise with a magnificent view of Diamond Head and Honolulu, room and private bath with a huge breakfast are only $35 per night.

Waikiki Circle Hotel, 2464 Kalakaua Avenue, 923-1571, right across from the beach with ocean views for most units, costs $39 to $45 with no kitchenettes.

Mid-priced ($50-$65 per night) condo bargains that have any charm are not easy to find without the help of first-rate management companies. One of the best is Donald R. Blum's Waikiki Beach Condominiums, which can be contacted in California at 213-541-8813. Ask about **444 Nahua**, 444 Nahua Street, just a few blocks from the heart of Waikiki.

My favorite splurge stay, near Diamond Head on an 800-foot white sand beach, is the **Kahala Hilton**. The

setting on Maunalua Bay is unsurpassed for an Oahu
resort and so are the restaurants (Maile, the Hala Terrace
for breakfast, and the Royal Hula Buffet). Try to reduce
the $180 per night by 50 percent in a package deal during
off-season.

Where to Eat
The variety of inexpensive, ethnic, exotic, enjoyable, and
outstanding restaurants in Waikiki compares with any city
of its size in the world. When you travel to Oahu's
beaches, mountaintops, or simply to the outskirts, take a
picnic lunch from a restaurant. Here's a sampling.

A local soup-to-nuts favorite (two locations, both open
24 hours) with good food, prices, and service is the
Wailana Coffee House, 1860 Ala Moana Boulevard and
2211 Kuhio Avenue (Outrigger Malia Hotel). Both have
validated parking.

Ono Hawaiian Foods, 726 Kapahulu Avenue, serves
the real thing for your first, or umpteenth, genuine
Hawaiian lunch or dinner. Nearby is **Keo's Thai Restaurant**, 625 Kapahulu; if you have a taste for superb Thai
delectables, you can't go wrong here.

Hee Hing, 449 Kapahulu Avenue, Diamond Head Center, qualifies as Hawaii's best decorated, best Cantonese
restaurant, with the biggest menu and most reasonable
prices. **Shirokiya**, 1450 Ala Moana Boulevard (upper
floor of Shirokiya Department Store in Ala Moana Center,
941-9111), is one of the best places in town to have Japanese food. The upper level is full of Japanese delicacies
that can be sampled, with intermittent Japanese arts and
crafts demonstrations.

Nightlife
Rascals, 2301 Kuhio Mall, 2nd Floor, 922-5566, has
multilevel disco until 4 a.m. **The Red Lion Dance
Palace's** disco-video system also keeps the dance floor
crowds until 4 a.m., at 240 Lewers Street; the **Blue Water
Seafood**, 2350 Kuhio Avenue (926-2191), has disco-
videos; **Garden Bar** and **La Mex** in the Royal Hawaiian

Shopping Center, 926-2000, offer entertainment nightly.
Or try low-key guitar playing at the **Seafood Empo-
rium**, 2201 Kala Kaua, Wednesday through Sunday
nights, 922-5547; **Trader Vic's**, daily, 923-1581; **Hawaiian Regent Hotel**, 922-6611, video dancing with two
dance floors, until 4 a.m.; **Hyatt Regency Waikiki**,
922-9292, at **Harry's Bar, Trappers**, and especially
disco at **Spats** until 4 a.m. nightly; the **Jazz Cellar,** 205
Lewers Street, 923-9952, with live rock and jazz until 4
a.m.; **Sheraton Moana Hotel**, 922-3111; the **Monarch
Room** at the **Royal Hawaiian Hotel**, 923-7311; and
Sheraton Princess Kaiulani, 922-5811, with nightly
entertainment. For up-to-date choices and information,
consult the free *This Week in Oahu*, a valuable guidebook found at all hotels.

Itinerary Options
Tantalus and Makiki Valley Trails: From Honolulu it is
three miles to Makiki Valley and six miles to Tantalus
Drive. Drive up Piikoi (past Ala Moana Center) to Mott-
Smith Drive, Makiki, and finally Tantalus, then three miles
up Tantalus to the trailhead. The trail is 1.1 miles one way.
 Beaches: Greater Honolulu has one pretty beach at
Diamond Head Beach Park, directly below the crater
and backed by cliffs. Snorkeling is good but not swimming, and the park usually swarms with tourists and, on
weekends, locals. For very pretty and superb beaches
that rival those on other islands, spend some time on the
windward coast, especially in the **Kailua, Lanikai**, and
Laie areas. In the Kaneohe area, **Kualoa County
Regional Park** has one of the finest white sand beaches
in the state with full facilities, and **Chinaman's Hat
Island** is within wading distance at low tide. In the
5,000-plus acres of **Kahana Valley State Park** north of
Kaneohe toward Laie, see its white sand beach and coconut grove fronting verdant Kahana Valley. Beautiful mile-
long **Malaekahana Bay Beach** is ideal for picnicking,
swimming, and snorkeling. Lovely (and privately owned)
Kakela and **Hukilau beaches** are both perfect for tent-

ing. **Malaekahana State Recreation Area**, especially
the beautiful hidden white sand paradise on the windward side of **Goat Island**, is worth visiting.

You probably would not want to try the bone-crushing
surf at **Sunset, Banzai**, and **Waimea beaches** on the
North Shore, especially in winter, but you'll certainly
want to see them, maybe picnic there and watch the daring surfers.

Seven miles west of Haleiwa is one of the loveliest
stretches of secluded beach in the state, **Mokuleia
Beach**, where I had the blessed good fortune to hike for
miles from my first home in Hawaii 30 years ago. It has
kept much of its original beauty. If you search for beaches
on the leeward side, with the Waianae Range in the background, keep going past **Makaha Beach** and **Keauu
Beach** north of Waianae to **Yokohama Bay**, a lovely
white sand beach at the end of Farrington Highway, with
windswept Kaena Point to the northwest and **Mokuleia
Beach** around the corner.

Cruises: See free local tourist magazines to clip discount coupons for dinner cruises. Most depart from the
Kewalo Basin Marina, near **Fisherman's Wharf,**
about 6:30 p.m. and return at 8:30 p.m., for $35 to $50
per person. Pearl Harbor cruises and sunset cruises and
Waikiki-Diamond Head cruises are offered by **Hawaiian
Cruises Ltd.,** 923-2061; sunset and dinner cruises can
be arranged with **Windjammer Cruises,** 521-0036.

Gliders, planes, and helicopters: The least expensive, most thrilling and serene way to see the island from
the air is in a glider. Drive out to the east coast past
Haleiwa and Mokuleia to Dillingham Air Force Base,
where the **Honolulu Soaring Club** (677-3434) offers
20- minute one- or two-passenger piloted glider rides for
$40 to $60 from 10:30 a.m. to 5:30 p.m. daily. Half-hour
plane rides for only $30 and an hour for $50, in Cessna
172s or 206s, are available from **Surf Air Tours,**
637-7003. Helicopter tours around the island range from
$40 quickies over Waikiki to tours of Oahu for $200 or
more per person. Contact: **Hawaii Pacific Helicopters,**

836-2071; **Kenai Air Hawaii,** 836-2071; and **Royal Helicopters,** 941-4683.

Game fishing: The waters offshore Oahu are full of ahi, ono, opakapaka, aku, mahi mahi, au, and marlin. The fishing charters moor at Kewalo Basin and include **Island Charters,** 536-7472; **Kono,** 531-0060; and **Sport Fishing Hawaii,** 536-6577.

Snorkeling and scuba diving: Both beginners and experienced divers have many choices around Oahu. **Hanauma Bay** (early in the morning) and **Sans Souci Beach** are best for novice divers and snorkelers. More experienced divers will try **Manana Island, Makapuu Point, Fantasy Reef** (off **Waialae Beach** at Kahala), **Laie Beach** (between Laie and Laniloa Point), and **Haleiwa Beach.** In summer (not in winter), experienced snorkelers will find a friendly assortment of fish at **Black Point, Waimea Beach, Sunset Beach, Pupukea Bay Beach, Kahe Beach Park,** and **Nanakuli Beach Park.** For diving equipment rental, contact: **Dan's Dive Shop,** 536-6181, next to Little George's restaurant on Ala Moana Boulevard; or **Waikiki Diving,** in two locations, 420 Nahua and 1734 Kalakaua, 922-7188. For snorkeling equipment rental, contact: **Fort DeRussy Beach Services,** 949-3469; **South Sea Aquatics,** 538-3854; or **Blue Water Snorkel,** 926-4485.

Surfing: Body-surf at **Makapuu Beach** beyond Koko Head beaches, Diamond Head end of **Prince** and **Kuhio beaches,** and **Kalama Beach** (Kailua) between Kalaka Place and Kaiona Place. Board-surf at **Waikiki Beach, Ala Moana Beach Park, Diamond Head Beach, Haleiwa Beach Park, Barbers Point, Chun's Reef, Pupukea, Banzai Pipeline, Kalama Beach, Makaha Beach, Yokohama Beach, Sunset Beach, Ehukai Beach Park,** and **Waimea Beach Park.** Contact: **Local Motion Surfboards,** 944-8515, **Waikiki Beach Services,** 923-3111, and the **Haleiwa Surf Center,** 637-5051.

Horseback riding: The two best areas for sightseeing by horseback are out of resorts: The **Sheraton Makaha Resort,** 695-9511, has rides up into the back reaches of

Waianae's Makaha Valley; and the **Turtle Bay Hilton,** 293-8811, has trails along the beautiful palm and iron-wood groves of deserted beaches on the northwest Kahuku tip.

Camping is permitted at three state campgrounds: **Keaiwa Heiau State Park; Malaekahana State Park** (supplemented by housekeeping cabins), on a beautiful white sandy beach on the east coast; and the **Sand Island State Campground** in Honolulu Harbor. There's a five-day limit and no camping on Wednesdays or Thursdays. Contact: Department of Land and Natural Resources, Division of State Parks, 548-7455. Camping is permitted at 15 county beach parks, Fridays through Wednesdays. The best campgrounds are at **Kahe, Kahuna Bay, Keaau, Lualualei, Mokuleia, Nanakuli, Punaluu,** and **Swanzy.**

Hiking opens up a different and more beautiful Oahu than you can see in any other way. Other islands attract more hikers, presumably because they are not as crowded, and Oahu has never sold itself as a place for hikers. Again, the predominant focus on Oahu is on Waikiki's hotels and beaches. About 25 percent of Oahu is owned by the military and closed to hikers. Likewise, a great deal of private land is posted against trespassing. There are no hikes on Oahu to compare with Kalalau on Kauai, in Haleakala Crater on Maui, or Mauna Loa on Hawaii. But overlooked are Oahu's outstanding shorter hikes to **Sacred Falls** and into **Makiki Valley.** There are other short hikes such as **Manoa Falls, Nuuana Valley** (Judd Memorial), **Blow Hole to Hanauma Bay, Waimano Trail, Diamond Head, Mauumae Trail, Makaha Valley, Koko Head Cliff Walk,** and **Makua Gulch.** The **Dupont Trail** to **Mt. Kaala** has good views from the highest point on Oahu (4,025 feet), but the final portion of the trail is too difficult and dangerous to recommend. You need a hiking permit from the Division of Forestry and a liability waiver from the owners, Waialua Sugar Company.

OAHU: PALI DRIVE AND WINDWARD COAST

Leave Waikiki for the windward coast's marvelous beaches and unusual parks and the Polynesian Cultural Center. Up over the Nuuanu Pali, with cliffs created by winds from the east and valleys like Nuuanu cut by streams from the west, to the windward side, you'll pass the Royal Mausoleum, Queen Emma's Summer Palace, and the Pali itself, where Kamehameha drove 16,000 enemy warriors to their deaths in his final victory to control the islands. Excellent beach parks line the windward shore.

Suggested Schedule

7:00 a.m.	Breakfast, swim, or jog on the beach.
8:30 a.m.	Drive to the Punchbowl.
9:30 a.m.	Drive up Pali Highway to Queen Emma's Summer Palace.
11:00 a.m.	Nuuanu Pali Lookout and some refreshments.
11:45 a.m.	Stop at Haiku Gardens.
12:30 p.m.	Tour the Valley of the Temples.
1:15 p.m.	Drive north on Highway 83 along the windward coast to Heeia State Park or Malaekahana Bay for a picnic lunch.
2:45 p.m.	Visit the Polynesian Cultural Center.
3:00 p.m.	See the "Pageant of the Long Canoes," followed by the Pacific Island exhibits.
7:00 p.m.	See "This Is Polynesia" dinner show.

Orientation

Lunalilo Highway (H1) runs north-south through Honolulu along the base of five major ridges, including Makiki Heights with Tantalus Drive, and five valleys, including Nuuanu Valley that flattens out to become the downtown. The Pali Highway (61) and Likelike Highway run from H1 east through these valleys between ridges to Kam Highway (83) on the windward side.

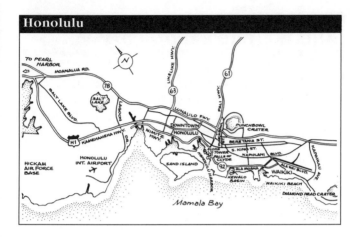

Sightseeing Highlights

▲▲▲The Pali Highway—Highway 61 through Nuuanu
Valley cuts across Oahu from Honolulu to the windward
coast, passing a series of the region's outstanding sightseeing attractions. The off-ramp into Nuuanu Valley
passes Queen Emma's Summer Palace, the royal retreat in
lush highlands in the late 1800s and now a museum.
Before the breathtaking overlook, turn onto Nuuanu Pali
Drive, which winds back to the highway.

▲▲The Punchbowl and the Royal Mausoleum—The
National Memorial Cemetery of the Pacific is on the
112-acre floor of a long-extinct volcano. The almost perfectly round Punchbowl Crater was called Puowaina (Hill
of Sacrifice) by the ancient Hawaiians. At the top of
Puowaina Drive at 2177 Puowaina Drive, 546-3190, the
Punchbowl is open 8 a.m. to 5:30 p.m. daily October
through March, 8 a.m. to 6:30 p.m. March through Sep-
tember. Take a moment to reflect on the price of war:
more than 30,000 service people are buried here and
over 26,000 are listed as missing in action. The lookout at
the top of the crater offers a great view of Honolulu. To
get there, take Punchbowl Avenue where it crosses King,
go under the freeway, and watch for signs to Punchbowl
Memorial. Take a right on Puowaina Street into the crater.

▲ **The Royal Mausoleum** contains the final resting place of every modern Hawaiian king and queen except King Kamehameha the Great and King William Lunalilo. Lydia Namahana Maioho, curator, and her son, William, will provide a memorable tour of this sacred place.

▲**Queen Emma's Summer Palace**—The wife of Kamehameha IV built her white frame house, now a museum, in the cool hills to escape the summer heat. This area was Honolulu's first suburb. Watch closely for the Pali Highway turnoff sign on the right so that you don't miss it. Admission $4, opens at 9 a.m., 595-3167, 2913 Pali Highway.

▲▲▲**The Nuuanu Pali Lookout**—You may have watched the sunset from here last evening, but this lookout also offers a magnificent morning view of windward Oahu in clear weather. Walk down to the old road for even better views.

▲▲ **Haiku Gardens**—Started in the mid-nineteenth century, the fruits, flowers, ornamental trees, pond, and landscaping have brought fame to this idyllic spot. The Haiku Gardens has a restaurant as an alternative to your beach picnic.

▲▲**The Valley of the Temples Memorial Park**—In Kaneohe, turn onto Kahekili Highway (83) north to the entrance to a beautifully landscaped cemetery set against a pali background, the **Byodo-In Temple.** A superb replica of a 900-year-old temple in Japan, this cemetery, its Japanese garden, and the majestic Byodo-In Temple make this one of the most unusual sites in all the islands and well worth a few dollars admission.

▲▲**The Laie Area**—Some of the state's best beaches are here. Three miles from Laie are **Sacred Falls,** where you can take an easy 2.2-mile hike to the pool beneath the waterfall. The water is cold, the area is beautiful and occasionally wet, and the mosquitoes are usually hungry.

▲▲**The Polynesian Cultural Center**—This cultural center in Laie is owned and operated by the Mormon church, which settled in this area in the mid-nineteenth century. The cultures of Hawaii, Fiji, Tonga, New Zealand,

Samoa, Tahiti, and the Marquesas are represented in
seven villages. You can take self-guided or guided walking
tours, tram rides, and canoe tours to watch poi-pounding,
basket weaving, woodcarving, and other crafts and par-
ticipate in native games. All village activity is performed
by young islanders attending the Brigham Young
University-Hawaii campus. (You can't miss the Mormon
Temple, white against the green pali.) The big events at
the Center are the 90-minute "This Is Polynesia" show
and "Pageant of the Long Canoes" with huge, costumed
casts, singing, dancing, stage scenery, and high-tech visual and sound effects. The admission charge for adults is
$38.95 and for children is $19.95 for all-day passes to see
everything and have the all-you-can-eat Gateway Buffet;
it is $6 more for the popular Alii Luau dinner. The dinner
show package alone is $34.95 for adults and $14.95 for
children. Without the dinner or show, the charge is
$24.95 for adults and $9.95 for children. Round-trip
motor coach transportation from the Royal Hawaiian
Shopping Center is $9 for adults, $5 for children. Watch
for special discounts that may be offered by tour opera-
tors or advertised in *This Week in Oahu*.

Where to Stay
The best deal on the windward coast is **The Countryside Cabins**, 53-224 Kamehameha Highway, Hauula, HI
96717, 237-8169, where Margaret Naai will put you in a
furnished studio for $30 per day or $180 per week.

Wendy Judy's **Akamai B&B** (263-0227) offers two
large studios in Kailua, with a pool and near the beach for
$59 per night or $340 per week, with special rates for
seniors. If Judy's is full, she'll fix you up at one of 26
other B&Bs.

Drive on Highway 61 through Kailua to Kalaheo Avenue
that runs along the coast. Pat O'Malley's **Pat's Kailua
Beach Properties**, 204 S. Kalaheo Avenue, Kailua, HI
96734, 261-1653 offers about 20 furnished cottages in a
beautiful setting overlooking Kailua Beach that cost from
$55 to $75 per day. (About 20 more of Pat's cottages and

houses cost more to rent.) Walk down Kailua Beach to
one of the most beautiful beaches in all of Hawaii,
Lanikai, two miles of paradise with only a few sunwor-
shipers except on weekends. Drive another 10 miles
north on Highway 83 to Laie and stay overnight for $70 to
$80 at the **Laniloa Lodge Hotel**, 55-109 Laniloa Street,
293-9282 next to the Polynesian Cultural Center. Nearby
on Laie Point is Oahu's most beautiful beach tucked in
the arm of the Point. This is an excellent base for visiting
Waimea Bay and Haleiwa attractions along with the Polynesian Cultural Center.

Where to Eat
The **Windward Mall Shopping Center** in Kaneohe,
like Ala Moana Shopping Center, provides most of the
inexpensive eating that you'll need in this part of the
island. The **Yummy Korea BBQ, Deli Express, Taco
Shop, Cinnabon's** cinnamon rolls, **Harpo's** excellent
deep-dish pizza, **Patti's Chinese Kitchen,** and **Little
Tokyo** offer variety and filling portions. If you drive to or
past Kahuku's Sugar Mill, the **Country Kitchen's** old-
fashioned calico bean soup and dessert will take care of
lunch until you reach the North Shore.
   Get all the fruit you can eat at the fruit stands on Route
83 just past Waiahole and Waikane. You can't beat the
prices and value of **Laniloa Lodge** right outside the gates
of the Polynesian Cultural Center for breakfast or lunch.
Beyond the Kahuku Mill Market Place on Kam Highway is
a tiny food stand—**Royal Hawaiian Shrimp and
Prawns**—with some of the best shrimp cocktail and
fried shrimp you've tasted.

Itinerary Options
After leaving the Byodo-In Temple, continue on Kam
Highway past Kaneohe to **Heeia State Park**, an ideal picnic site on a beautiful small peninsula overlooking Heeia
Fishpond, one of the few left on the island and the
largest. Return to Kam Highway heading north and look
for the turnoff on the left (Pulama Road) to **Senator**

Fong's Plantation and Gardens. A 40-minute narrated tram ride through the plantation's beautiful acreage (9 a.m.-4 p.m.) costs adults $6.50, children 5 to 12, $3. Brief stops at **Kahana Bay Beach Park** or **Punalu'u Beach Park** for a swim can follow exploration of the 5,220 acres of **Kahana Valley State Park** and its hiking trails. Now you're ready to move on to the **Laie Area**, the **Malaekahana State Recreation Area**, the **Kahuku Sugar Mill**, and **Kahuku Mill Market Place**, all on Kam Highway heading toward the North Shore. The renovated mill is open for shopping and tours, which include fresh sugarcane to suck and chew.

▲▲**Malaekahana State Recreation Area**—Full of palm, ironwood, and hala trees with a lovely beach where camping is allowed with a state permit. There are rustic beachfront cabins for rent at $25 per night, 293-1736. Bring your own bedding and cooking gear. The windward side of nearby Goat Island, a bird sanctuary, has one of the most beautiful white sand beaches in the state. You can reach it by wading across the reef during low tide.

OAHU: NORTH SHORE TO
DOWNTOWN HONOLULU

The North Shore is world famous for its legendary surfing beaches. In the winter, gaze in awe at Sunset, Ehukai, and Banzai beaches, and Waimea Bay (calm as a lake in summer). Drive up Pupukea Road for the spectacular view of the North Shore from Puu O Mahuka Heiau. Visit beautiful Waimea Falls Park. After lunch in Haleiwa or on Mokuleia Beach, return to downtown Honolulu with a brief stop at the Wahiawa Botanic Garden. Spend the rest of the afternoon exploring historic and restored sections of Honolulu before dinner in Chinatown.

Suggested Schedule

7:00 a.m.	Swim before breakfast?
8:00 a.m.	Breakfast and depart for North Shore.
10:00 a.m.	Waimea Falls Park or farther north to surfing beaches.
12:00 noon	Lunch at the Proud Peacock in Waimea Falls Park or in Haleiwa.
1:00 p.m.	Drive on Highway 99 through the pineapple and sugarcane fields to Honolulu.
1:30 p.m.	Explore the Bishop Museum.
3:30 p.m.	Brief look at Aliiolani Hale, Iolani Palace, Washington Place, St. Andrews Cathedral, Kawaiahao Church, the Mission Houses Museum and its excellent gift shop.
4:30 p.m.	Visit the Hawaii Maritime Center and watch the sunset over Honolulu from Aloha Tower.
6:30 p.m.	Dinner in Chinatown.
8:00 p.m.	Another swing through Waikiki's nightlife.

Sightseeing Highlights
▲ **Sunset, Ehukai, Banzai Pipeline, and Waimea Bay**—Surfing beaches here, for experts only from November through February, are fairly safe for swimming at other times of year.

▲▲ **Puu O Mahuka Heiau**—This was probably the site of human sacrifices in the precolonization period. The view of Waimea Beach is outstanding.

▲▲▲**Waimea Falls Park**—This is a privately owned 1,800- acre nature reserve. The entrance is several miles into a lush valley that was once inhabited by thousands of Hawaiians. Primarily a botanical garden, the park includes entertainment such as hula dancers and divers who plunge 55 feet into the pool below the falls. You can swim at the base of the falls, walk on beautiful trails, or just stroll around the central meadow's **Waimea Arboretum and Botanical Gardens** with or without a free guided tour. You'll also see some species of Hawaiian wildlife including nene geese, "Kona nightingales" (wild donkeys), and wild boar. For visitors to the islands, admission charges are: $11.95 adults, $6.50 children 7 to 12, and $2.25 children 4 to 6. The park is open from 10 a.m. to 5:30 p.m., 639-8511. On weekends, the park can be quite crowded, but trails up the hillsides offer an escape. Ride the open-air tram to the top of the valley and walk down. Spend the whole day, if possible, and during full moon take a moonlight walk before dining at Proud Peacock restaurant (closes at 9 p.m.).

▲▲ **Haleiwa**—This is still a plantation town with old character despite many new shops. Haleiwa Beach Park is safe for swimming year-round. Route 82 from Haleiwa continues along the coast to **Mokuleia,** near Dillingham Airfield, which has a long stretch of secluded beach. You can hike all the way down to Kaena Point and around to the Waianae Coast and Yokohama Beach.

▲▲▲**Bishop Museum**—This museum at 1525 Bernice Street, 847-3511, contains the most complete collection of historical displays on Hawaii and Polynesia in the world. Be sure to see the Hall of Hawaiian Natural History. Admission is $5.95 for adults and $4.95 for children 6-17. Museum hours: 9 a.m. to 5 p.m. Monday through Saturday and the first Sunday of every month, Family Sunday, with food booths, craft displays, and entertainment. To get there, take exit 20A off H1 to Route 63. Quickly get

into the right lane for a right turn on Bernice Street. Or,
bus #2 lets you off two blocks from the museum on
Kapalama Street.

▲▲ **Downtown Honolulu**—King Kamehameha's statue
here is one of three. In front of the **Aliiolani Hale,** it is a
duplicate made to replace the original, which was lost at
sea en route from Paris. It was found much later in a Port
Stanley junkyard and erected in Kapaau not far from the
king's birthplace. Aliiolani Hale (The Judiciary Building),
at King and Mililani streets, was supposed to be a palace,
but Kamehameha V, who commissioned it, died before
its completion and it was converted to a court building.
Iolani Palace was completed in 1882 and used as a royal
palace for only 17 years.

To the left of Washington Place is **St. Andrews Cathedral,** built in 1867 of stone shipped from England. In
front is the **Hawaii State Capitol. Kawaiahao Church,**
at South King and Punchbowl streets, was built in 1841
out of coral quarried from local reefs. The **Mission
Houses Museum** on King Street across from the church
includes the oldest wooden structure in Hawaii, precut
and shipped from Boston in 1819, as well as the first
printing press west of the Rockies. It's open daily and
charges $3.50. The gift shop has an excellent collection
of Hawaiiana. The museum also offers a two-hour walking tour of Honolulu.

▲▲ **The Hawaii Maritime Center** consists of three
attractions. Aloha Tower on Pier 9, at ten stories the tallest
building in town when it was built in 1926, still com-
mands excellent views of the harbor and city. The *Falls of
Clyde* on Pier 7, built in Scotland in 1878, is the world's
only full-rigged, four-masted ship. The *Hokuke'a*, an
authentic replica of an ancient Polynesian double-hulled
sailing canoe, made a 5,000-mile round-trip to Tahiti in
1976. Open daily 9 a.m. to 5 p.m., $6 adults, $3 ages 6 to
17, under 6 free (536-6373).

▲▲ **Chinatown**—On the eastern fringe of downtown
between Nuuanu Avenue, North Beretania Street, and
South King Street, this part of town is both modern and

rundown (the whole district burned down in 1900). The pagoda of Wo Fat's at the corner of Hotel and Maunakea streets is a good starting point for a tour. The most interesting stores are on **Maunakea Street** between Hotel and King streets: little Chinese groceries, herb shops dispensing ancient medications like ground snakeskin and powdered monkey brain, jewelry shops, ceramic shops, acupuncture supplies, and import stores. Also note the art galleries on Nuuanu, Smith, and Maunakea streets. Combine visiting a gallery, such as the Bakkus Gallery, Gateway Gallery, or Pegge Hopper Gallery on Nuuana, and lunch at one of the restaurants below. Try a piece of lotus root candy. The island end of Maunakea Street is bounded by the **Cultural Plaza,** designed to exhibit Hawaii's multicultural makeup. Nearby is the People's Open Market, a cooperative of open-air stalls.

Where to Eat
North Shore
The **Proud Peacock** in Waimea Falls Park is a very special place to have lunch or dinner surrounded by gardens, with peacocks roaming about. **Steamers** in Haleiwa Shopping Plaza serves great appetizers and vegetarian or fish dishes on an outdoor lanai. Sunday brunch (10 a.m.-3 p.m.) is the best way to start Sunday on the North Shore. **Pizza Bob's**, Haleiwa Shopping Plaza, has really tasty pizzas. **Jameson's by the Sea**, Kamehameha Highway, 637-4336, near Haleiwa, has an excellent seafood menu, and you can watch the sunset. **Matsumoto's Grocery** in Haleiwa has shave ice—fine frosty particles bathed in one of two dozen possible syrups, including delicious mango and pineapple.

The **Café Haleiwa**, 66-460 Kamehameha Highway, 637-5561, a tiny place on the left as you enter Haleiwa, serves excellent and cheap breakfasts with names like "Surf Rat" and "Dawn Patrol," in honor of the café's hungry après-surfing clientele. Early-bird specials from 6 to 7 a.m.

Honolulu

In 1986, **Wo Fat's**, 115 Hotel Street, 537-6260, celebrated its 100th anniversary as Honolulu's premier Chinese restaurant. **Sea Fortune**, next door to Wo Fat's, at 111 King Street, is a dim sum dream. **Yung's Kitchen** at 1170 Nuuanu Avenue is practically next door to Pegge Hopper's gallery, closes at 11:30 p.m., and serves some of Hawaii's best Chinese dishes in a no-frills dining room. **Won Kee Seafood Restaurant**, Chinese Cultural Plaza, 100 N. Beretania Street, will stretch your budget a bit with every imaginable seafood dish—fried, steamed, baked, marinated, or otherwise Won Kee'd—but the result is one of the very best in the state. **Kyo-ya Restaurant**, 2057 Kalakaua Avenue, 947-3911, combines gracious friendliness, atmosphere, excellent food, and moderate prices. **Food Courts** at Ala Moana's Makai Market, International Marketplace in Waikiki, and Windward Mall on Kam Highway in Kaneohe are the best around for a variety of budget food: Mexican, Hawaiian, Korean, Chinese, Japanese, Thai, Italian, and American. Most meals are under $5 and filling.

Itinerary Options

The **USS Arizona Memorial** in Pearl Harbor is in a very special category as a sightseeing attraction. The hull of the USS *Arizona* is the tomb of 1,102 men who died in Japan's surprise attack on December 7, 1941. The shrine can be visited in two ways: on an excursion boat, which can't land at the memorial, and by land, which can be crowded but more informative. Catch a #4 shuttle bus from Waikiki, 926-4747, or TheBus #50 directly to the site where a free shuttle boat ferries you out to the *Arizona* Memorial. Or drive from Waikiki's Kalakaua Avenue to Ala Moana Boulevard to Nimitz Highway (West 92) to H1 West to Highway 90 to USS *Arizona* Memorial Visitor Center, and then take a launch to the memorial. Admission is $6 for adults, $1 for children 6 to 12.

Explore the **Leeward** or **Waianae Coast** running 20 miles from Barbers Point to Kaena Point, with Farrington Highway (93) paralleling the coastline. In Waianae, turn onto Waianae Valley Road for **Pokai Bay Beach Park,** a sheltered bay with a calm, safe swimming beach. Drive on to **Makaha** to visit the Sheraton Makaha Resort and Country Club, horseback ride in the beautiful valley, have a drink by the pool or dinner at the Kaala Room. At the desk, arrange to see the **Kaneaki Heiau** in Makaha Valley, the most complete reconstruction of a temple besides the City of Refuge on the Big Island's south Kona Coast. Continue on to **Yokohama Bay** and **Kaena Point State Park** for hiking, picnicking, and viewing the magnificent **Waianae Mountains.**

MAUI: EXPLORING THE NORTHWEST COAST

After an early morning departure from Honolulu, head directly from Maui's airport to Lahaina for a full morning of sightseeing. After lunch at one of Lahaina's waterfront restaurants, drive north along coastal Highway 30 to Kapalua. Spend the afternoon at the coconut palm-fringed Kapalua Beach. Drive up to Pineapple Hill for refreshments on the patio while watching the sunset against a panoramic ocean view. Drive back to Lahaina to get ready for dinner and a night out in Lahaina or, if you plan to see the sunrise from Haleakala's summit, head for bed right after dinner in order to leave Lahaina tomorrow by 3 a.m.

Suggested Schedule

6:00 a.m.	Snack breakfast, check out of hotel, and head for the airport.
7:30 a.m.	Fly from Honolulu to Kahului Airport, Maui.
8:03 a.m.	Arrive in Maui and rent car (or take Gray Line Maui's shuttle from the airport to Lahaina) and check in.
9:15 a.m.	Breakfast in Lahaina.
9:45 a.m.	Walking tour of Lahaina harbor and town.
1:00 p.m.	Lunch on Front Street in Lahaina.
2:00 p.m.	Drive up the coast to Kapalua.
2:30 p.m.	Afternoon swimming and snorkeling at Kapalua Beach.
5:00 p.m.	Refreshments on the patio at Pineapple Hill, Kapalua Resort.
7:30 p.m.	Dinner in Lahaina.
9:00 p.m.	Lahaina or Kaanapali Resort nightlife, or early to bed and early to rise for a sunrise trip to Haleakala.

Getting to Maui
The recently built Kahului Airport receives flights from
Aloha Airlines, Hawaiian Air, Aloha Interisland Air, Ameri-
can, Delta, and United.

Transportation
There's no public bus system on Maui, so you'll need a
car to get around. Reserve a car in advance. Ask whether
the company has a pickup service at the airport. You'll
find an abundance of local car rental companies, more
than on any other island, with cars for $21 to $25 per day,
flat rate with unlimited mileage.

Rent a car right at the airport or get a free ride to car
rental offices nearby. In the airport are Alamo Rent-A-Car,
877-3466; American International Rent-A-Car, 877-7604;
Andres Rent-A-Car, 877-5378; Avis Rent-A-Car, 877-5167;
Budget Rent-A-Car, 871-8811; Dollar Rent-A-Car, 871-8811;
Hertz Rent-A-Car, 877-5167; Pacific Rent-A-Car, 877-3065;
Robert's Rent-A-Car, 871-6226; and Trans-Maui Rent-A-
Car, 877-5222. Outside the airport, older model used
cars can be rented at Rent-A-Wreck, 800-367-5230;
Uptown Service, 244-0869; and Word of Mouth Rent-A-
Used-Car, 877-2436. Other car rental companies include
Kamaaina, 877-5460; Maui Car Rental and Leasing,
877-2081; National Car Rental, 877-5347; Sunshine Rent-
A-Car, 871-6222; Thrifty Car Rental, 871-7596; and Tropi-
cal Rent-A-Car, 877-0002.

Grayline, 877-5507, has a shuttle service from Kahului
to Lahaina-Kaanapali for about $9.50 per person, Trans-
Hawaiian Services, 877-7308, provides a shuttle service
that stops running at 5 p.m.

Sightseeing Highlights
▲▲▲ **Lahaina**—This was the political center of the
Hawaiian kingdom from about 1800 to 1945. Around
1820, the town became the main provisioning stop for
whaling ships and the playground for thousands of seamen and quickly lost its innocence. About the same time,
missionaries arrived for a classic confrontation between

Maui

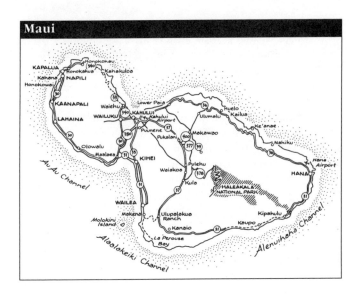

salvation and sin. In 1962, Lahaina was designated a
National Historic Landmark. In the same year, the Lahaina
Restoration Foundation was formed to restore the
historic sites along Front Street. The rapidly growing collection of shops, galleries, restaurants, and other attractions draws millions of visitors annually and produces
traffic jams and parking problems. Lahaina now stretches
2 ½ miles, four blocks deep. The heart of the town is a
one-third mile stretch between Shaw and Papalaua
streets. Front Street, the main shopping and entertainment strip, runs between these streets.

The Cannery, a large air-conditioned shopping mall
opened in 1987 in a former pineapple cannery and
located on Highway 30 as you leave Lahaina, recently was
joined by another 150,000 square feet of shopping mall
extending between Front Street and Highway 30.
Altogether, Lahaina shopping space far exceeds Ala Moana
on Oahu and is approaching Waikiki. Where or when will
it stop?

Be sure to stop at the **Lahaina Printsellers** on Front
Street in the historic Seamen's Hospital to see a remark-

able collection of real antique prints and old maps, and the **Village Gallery** (the Cannery and 120 Dickenson Street, Lahaina; the Embassy Suites, Kaanapali), which displays the two- and three-dimensional work of many of Maui's best artists. The historic places to see are within a few blocks of Front Street:

The **Banyan Tree**, planted behind the courthouse on April 24, 1873, by Sheriff William Owen Smith to commemorate the 50th anniversary of Lahaina's first Protestant mission, is the largest in the islands, covering about two-thirds of an acre. On the harbor side of the Banyan Tree are the coral stone ruins of the Old Fort constructed in the 1830s to protect missionaries' homes from whalers.

The Pioneer Inn, built in 1901, had the only accommodations in west Maui until the late 1950s. Across Papelekane Street is the Brick Palace, the first Western-style building in the islands, built by Kamehameha I. Across from the Pioneer Inn on Front Street is the **Baldwin Home Museum**, the New England-style residence with furnishings of medical missionary Dwight Baldwin, whose offspring became some of the largest landowners in the islands.

Carthaginian II, anchored in the harbor directly opposite the Pioneer Inn, is a two-masted square-rigged replica of the ship that went aground in 1920. It contains a museum exhibit of the whaling era. Open from 9 a.m. to 4:30 p.m. Admission is $2 for adults; accompanied children are admitted free.

Waiola Church, the first stone church in the islands (circa 1830), has been rebuilt several times, the latest in 1953, when the name was changed from "Wainee" in an attempt to change its luck. Waiola Cemetery behind the church dates back to 1823. Many Hawaiian chiefs and queens who became Christians are buried there.

Wo Hing Society Hall on Front Street, built in 1912 by Chinese laborers imported to the island, has a small museum and social hall. **Lahaina Jodo Mission** at 12 Ala Moana Street, founded in 1921, contains the 12-foot bronze and copper giant Buddha cast in Japan and sent to

Maui in 1968 for a centennial celebration of the first Japanese immigrants to Hawaii.

▲▲**Kaanapali Resort**—Starting four miles north of Lahaina, this is the beginning of the west Maui Gold Coast that continues ten miles to Kapalua. The 500-acre resort contains seven hotels, including the new Embassy Suites, five condominium complexes, two golf courses, a shopping center, and miles of sandy beaches. Beyond Kaanapali are the condominium "villages" of Honokowai, Kahana, Napili, and Kapalua. Highway 30 (the Hono a Piilani Highway) circles west Maui.

Visit the **Whalers Village Museum** on the third floor of **Whalers Village Shopping Center** (9:30 a.m.-9:30 p.m., closed 1-1:30 p.m.) to see a unique display of whaling artifacts and photos and a 30-minute whale video shown every half hour.

The best place to swim and snorkel in the Kaanapali Resort is next to **Black Rock** (Pu'u Keka'a) at the Sheraton Hotel's beach. The great mid-eighteenth-century king-warrior, Kahikili, leaped from this ancient "leaping place" of souls into their ancestral spiritland, a leap reenacted nightly by divers from the hotel.

▲**"Sugar Cane Train" (Lahaina-Kaanapali & Pacific Railroad)**—An oil-fired narrow-gauge steam locomotive (Anaka or Myrtle), refurbished to resemble a vintage sugarcane locomotive, carries you in an open passenger car on a six-mile excursion past golf courses, cane fields, and ocean views. The train makes five 25-minute (one-way) trips daily between the Puukolii Boarding Platform (across from the Royal Lahaina) and the Lahaina Station, with a stop at the Kaanapali Station. A one-way ticket is $6, round-trip $9.

Where to Stay
If you have a car, anywhere in the Lahaina, Kaanapali, Honokowai, and Napili Bay area can serve as a base for the day or the entire stay on Maui. You could spend the second night on Maui in Kahului to be about 22 miles and 40 minutes closer to Hana, but it's not too far to come back to west Maui that night, too.

The highest-priced accommodations are in Kaanapali and Kapalua; next is Kahana, with a resort atmosphere and mostly high-rise condos. The undeveloped beach-front planted with sugarcane between Kaanapali and Honokowai, the old Kaanapali Airport, very soon will be developed into an extension of the Kaanapali Resort. This leaves Honokowai's mix of older and newer, high- and low-rise condos as the only "moderate" priced collection of vacation units ($60-$100).

On the wharf overlooking the Lahaina harbor, the land-mark **Pioneer Inn**, 658 Wharf Street, Lahaina 96761, 661-3636, or Honolulu 949-4121, offers simple rooms with ceiling fans and plenty of atmosphere, all with private bath, mostly with queen beds and a twin, at $36 single in the old wing and $60 single or double in the new wing, which has private baths, lanais, and air-conditioning.

In Lahaina, my favorite inn/B&B, featuring Victorian decor with pedestal bathroom sinks and poster beds, is the **Plantation Inn** (built in 1987), offering 8 double rooms, a suite, and a three-bedroom cottage. All deluxe, the rates start at $95 per room with breakfast. The inn is one of a kind and right near the heart of town. **Gerard's** restaurant occupies the front of the building and guests receive a 20 to 40 percent discount on dinners, which offsets the high room cost.

A one-bedroom garden unit ($65) at the **Maui Sands**, 3559 Lower Hono a Piilani, Lahaina, 669-4811 (or 800-367-55037), is one of the best budget accommodations in Honokowai.

You pay more for newer oceanside units, more luxuri-ous furnishings, and lanais with views. The older **Honokowai Palms**, 3666 Lower Hono a Piilani High-way, Lahaina 96761, 669-6130, is across the street from the beach with one-bedroom oceanview units, or two-bedroom apartments without ocean view, for two at $65.

Best value for the money in the Napili area is the **Coco-nut Inn**, 181 Hui Road, Napili, 96761, 800-367-8006 or 669-5712. Forty-one units on two levels are tucked in a

lovely garden setting (with pool and hot tub) away from
the main road on a hill overlooking Napili. Comfortable
studio units for two with kitchen and tub/shower cost
$79 including a delicious continental breakfast. Also try
Napili Sunset, 46 Hui Road (669-8083, 800-421-0680),
right on Napili Bay if their $88 units are available.

Where to Eat
In Lahaina, the deck at **Kimo's**, 845 Front Street,
661-4811, is the "in" spot for excellent waterfront lunches
and dinners, but the view of Lanai and Molokai is expensive. For less crowds and lower prices, try breakfast of the
best coconut, banana, or macadamia nut pancakes or a
lunch of seafood chowder on the terrace of the Pioneer
Inn's **Harpooner's Lanai**, 658 Wharf Street.

Croissant and brioche come warm from the ovens of
The Bakery at 991 Limahina Place, near the Sugar Cane
Train Depot. Also on the Kaanapali side of town, **Lahaina
Natural Foods**, 1295 Front Street, has fresh baked goods,
a very good deli, and great sandwiches to take out.

Greenthumb's, 839 Front Street, 667-6126, on the
decks of the old fishing house, is a delightful garden café
with a good variety of light and inexpensive home-style
lunches and dinners, with plenty of salad. Another inexpensive restaurant for lunch on the waterfront is the
Organ Grinder Restaurant, 811 Front Street, 661-4593.

Hamburger Mary's, 608 Front Street, 667-6989, a
lovely garden restaurant, has great breakfast deals, filling
soup and salad lunches, and an assortment of huge ham-
burgers and sandwiches.

Take out an Italian picnic lunch for the beach from
Longhi's Pizzeria Deli, 930 Wainee Street.

A gourmet splurge dinner or lunch in the courtyard of
charming **Gerard's**, located in the extraordinary Plantation Inn, 174 Lahainaluna Road (661-8939), is one of the
outstanding dining experiences in Hawaii. Chef Gerard
Reversade creatively changes his menus daily, and all of
the beef, veal, duck, chicken, seafood, and other sur-

prises are superbly prepared with the freshest ingredients
and elegant sauces. Five miles south of Lahaina, about a
ten-minute drive, **Chez Paul**, 820-B Olowalu Village,
661-3843, has two seatings (6:30 p.m. and 8:30 p.m.) for
excellent French cuisine.

Ricco's, 661-4433, in the Whaler's Village complex,
offers buffet platters and a variety of excellent subs that
qualify as family budget meals.

Between Kahana and Kapalua, the very best restaurant
stop for atmosphere, location, and view is the **Seahouse
Restaurant**, 669-6271, at Napili Kai Beach Club on Napili
Bay. Situated at the end of the beach, the open-air dining
room and bar is the place to come after a swim at Napili
or Kapalua Beach (just a short walk over the hill) and
watch the sunset over drinks or dinner. A gourmet lunch
at **The Market Cafe**, 669-4888, in the Kapalua Shopping
Plaza, offers outstanding wine, beer, cheese, coffee, and
dessert selections at surprisingly reasonable prices. Or
plan a predinner drink watching the sun sink over
Molokai from the renowned patio of **Pineapple Hill**,
669-6129, set high above Kapalua's beachfront resort.

Surprisingly, some of the best dinner values can be
found at dinner buffets at the big resorts, especially during summer months. Especially check out the seafood or
regular buffet at the **Westin Maui** and the **Marriott's
Moano Terrace** next door at Kaanapali.

Nightlife
Strolling around Lahaina and people-watching between
shopping, eating, and pub-crawling is entertainment
enough. In addition, Lahaina's bars around Front Street
and in the shopping complexes have all the music and
activity you want. The **Lahaina Broiler** hops until mid-
night. Disco at **Moose McGillicuddy's** nightly. On
weekends, it's Hawaiian music at the **Banyan Inn**, jazz at
Blackie's Bar, and dancing at **Longhi's** on Friday and
Saturday nights. The $22 luau and cocktail or $36 dinner
show ("Drums of the Pacific") at **Hyatt Regency** is one
of the best in Kaanapali. Disco at the Hyatt's **Spats II** is

one of the most popular on the island (open to 4 a.m.). Before or after, you can walk around the hotel's public areas to window-shop and view the displays of Oriental art. The disco at the Maui Marriott, the **Banana Moon**, is open until 1:30 a.m. and may be to your liking.

Itinerary Options
You haven't seen Maui without checking out the grounds and interiors of the **Hyatt Regency** and **Westin Maui** at Kaanapali, **Kapalua Bay, Stouffer Wailea Bay**, and **Four Seasons** in Wailea, and the **Maui Prince Resort** at nearby Makena. By 1992, the new **Ritz Carlton** in Kapalua should be open. And each of these resorts has expensive, touristy shopping that also is part of the experience.

Lahaina is a center for **water sports activities** — cruises, sailing, snorkeling, scuba diving, fishing, and whale-watching. Arrange for any of these activities at the **Lahaina Beach Center**, 661-5959, or the **Lahaina Sea Sport Center**, 667-2759. For about $35, you can take either the *Kaulana*, a 70-foot motor-powered catamaran, 667-2518, or the three-masted schooner *Spirit of Windjammer*, Windjammer Cruises, 667-6834 or 800-843-8113, with dinner and open bar.

Deep-sea fishing for marlin, yellowfin tuna, mahimahi, and other local fish runs about $65 a half day on a share basis and $125 to $150 for an eight-hour day at **Aerial Sportfishing**, 667-9089; **Lahaina Charter Boats**, 667-6672; and **Aloha Activity Center**, 667-9564.

Whale-watching excursions from January through April leave Lahaina Harbor in the morning and afternoon and cost $20 for an adult. Contact **Seabird Cruises**, 661-3643, or **Windjammer Cruises**, or book a cruise through the **Pacific Whale Foundation,** 879-6530. The price is $25 for adults, $12.50 for children 3 to 12. Check the Whale Report Center, 661-8527, for the latest report on whale sightings.

Snorkel at the Sheraton, next to Black Rock. Park at the Whaler's Shopping Center to walk to the beach. (The

Sheraton parking lot actually has a few spaces reserved for beach users.) Better still, drive out Highway 30 to **Honolua Bay** (except in winter), walk a few hundred yards, and try the best snorkeling on Maui. Otherwise, half-day excursions, with lunch or breakfast, to **Molokini Crater,** the remainder of a volcano (eight miles and visible from **Maalaea Harbor**) are $50 round-trip (max.) for adults, $12 for children.

Dive packages to Molokai and Lanai or just offshore cost from $70 to $100 through **American Dive of Maui**, 661-4885; **Central Pacific Divers**, 661-8718 or 800-551-6767; **Dive Maui**, 667-2080; **Hawaiian Reef Divers,** 667-7647; **Lahaina Divers,** 667-7496; and **Scuba Schools of Maui**, 661-8036. Snorkelers, contact **Maui Adventures,** 661-3400, or **Snorkeling Hawaii,** 661-8156, for two-hour cruises out of Lahaina at about $20 per person.

Surfing is best in the summer at Lahaina and Kaanapali. Check with **Lahaina Dive & Surf**, 667-6001. Otherwise, for experienced surfers, Honolua Bay and Hookipa Beach Park on the North Shore, and Hamoa Beach in Hana, are the best spots on Maui.

If you have extra time, drive around the **West Maui Mountains**. Make sure you have a full gas tank. Driving from Kapalua to Wailuku, only 18 miles, takes three hours. Route 330 changes to Route 340 at Honokohau Bay and becomes a rutted dirt road that your car rental agency hates; they will not accept responsibility for car damage. (Check first to see if the road is passable or washed out, which happens. Actually, you're following an old royal horse trail.) Pass picturesque **Kahakuloa**, cliffs, valleys, and lush fern gulches between razor-backed ridges that run from Puu Kukui's mile-high summit to the sea. After the road becomes paved again in the cane plantation town of Waihee, a side road leads up to **Halekii Heiau**, once football field-size temples, now rubble.

Helicopter tours are very expensive and thrilling. If you can let go of your pocketbook for $90 to $280 (depending on the season) to see west Maui, Haleakala, Hana, the whole island, or Molokai, it's well worth it.

Flightseeing excursions with **Papillon Helicopters**, 800-367-7095 or 669-4884, depart from the Pineapple Hill Helipad near Kapalua, fly over the West Maui Mountains, and land in a wilderness spot for a champagne picnic. Papillon also has a flight that will get you to Haleakala for sunrise, followed by a visit to Hana.

MAUI: HALEAKALA VOLCANO AND UPCOUNTRY

Haleakala ("House of the Sun"), the world's largest dormant volcano, a "Mt. Everest" in the Pacific, rises from 20,000 feet under the sea to over 10,000 feet above sea level. As the sun rises or sets, its light paints pastel streaks on the massed clouds and edges the crater's vast rim in red and golden hues. Only high priests and sorcerers dared to reside in this spellbinding place. Today, 63 miles from Lahaina, you visit the summit of Haleakala National Park, preferably at sunrise, and hike some of the crater's shorter trails before descending to the volcano's lower slopes—upcountry.

Suggested Schedule

3:00 a.m.	Phone for weather report: 572-7749. Then head east on Highway 378 to Haleakala. (Too early? Then leave at 6:00 and arrive at the summit way too late for sunrise.)
5:30 a.m.	Park Headquarters and then Puu Ulaula Visitor's Center at Haleakala summit for sunrise or early morning views.
6:30 a.m.	Snack breakfast at summit before venturing out on the crater trails.
7:00 a.m.	Walk on Halemauu or Sliding Sands Trail.
10:00 a.m.	Return to Visitor's Center to see exhibits and hear talk by ranger.
12:00 noon	Descend for lunch in upcountry.
2:00 p.m.	Browsing and shopping in Makawao and Paia.
3:30 p.m.	Kula Botanical Gardens.
4:30 p.m.	Tedeschi Winery for winetasting.
6:00 p.m.	Sunset from Kula (or as an option, on Haleakala).
7:00 p.m.	Dinner in Makawao and overnight in the upcounty.

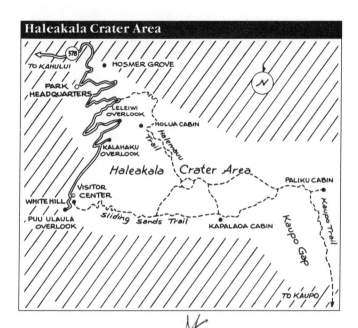

Haleakala Crater Area

Sightseeing Highlights

▲▲▲ **Haleakala**—This eerie pyramid of incredibly
dense volcanic rock has a 3,000-foot-deep crater dwarf-
ing nine cinder cone mountains across its floor, including
thousand-foot-high Puu O Maui. Frequently, misty
clouds surround the 7½-mile-long, 2½-mile-wide crater, obscuring its 21 miles of rim from view.

Before starting the 2½-hour drive from Lahaina (1½
hours from Kahului) to the summit of Haleakala, phone
for a taped report on weather and travel conditions. Start
early because clouds begin rolling in by 9:00 or 10:00
a.m. *Dress warmly* (sweaters or parka), especially for sunrise and sunset excursions. Prepare to freeze and fry.
Bring insulated clothing, a blanket and mittens, rain gear
and sun protection, including hats and sunscreen, lunch
and plenty of liquids, as well as cameras, plenty of film,
and binoculars.

From Kahului, go southeast on Highway 37 about 10
miles to Pukalani, then turn east (left) on Highway 377.

After 6 miles of climbing through cane and then pineapple fields, turn east again onto Highway 378, which snakes 12 miles to Park Headquarters through pastures and rocky wastelands at higher elevations. It's over 10 miles from Park Headquarters to the summit. Drive carefully on the many switchbacks.

At **Halemauu Trail** (8,000 feet), walk a mile to the crater rim, where you can see the trail zigzagging down the crater wall, or wait until you reach the Leleiwi Overlook for the same view closer to the road. At Kalahaku Overlook you'll see silverswords, the Hawaii state flower that takes 4 to 20 years to bloom once (sometime from May through October) and then dies.

Two visitor's shelters await at the summit: the **Haleakala Visitor's Center** on the rim has exhibits and hourly talks explaining the region's geology and legends; and the glass-enclosed **Puu Ulaula Visitor's Center** on the summit (Red Hill), where you see the unforgettable sunrises or sunsets, is an easy quarter-mile hike past stone shelters and sleeping platforms used by Hawaiians who came up to quarry iron-hard stone for tools.

After spending all the time you want on the summit, go down inside the crater. **Sliding Sands**, the main crater trail, starts near the Visitor's Center. (You can return to the road via Halemauu Trail, hitching back to the summit.) As you descend Sliding Sands Trail, through cinders and ash, you can see the contrasting lush forests of the Koolau Gap. It's about four miles to the crater floor.

On the drive down, stop a mile past the park entrance at **Hosmer Grove** (7,030 feet) for a walk on the nature trail through cedar, spruce, juniper, pines, and trees imported from Australia, India, and Japan.

▲▲▲**Upcountry**—This area encircles Haleakala from Haiku and the cowboy town of Makawao to Kula, Poli Poli State Park above Kula, and out Highway 37 to the **Ulupalakua Ranch** and the **Tedeschi Winery**, part of the 37,000-acre ranch. The rich volcanic soil of Kula makes it Maui's flower and vegetable garden spot. Descending Highway 378, turn left on Highway 377 to the **Kula Botanical Gardens**, which displays more than 700 types of plants, open 9 a.m. to 4 p.m., adults $2.50, 878-1715. On Highway 378, one mile past Sunrise Market, is **Sunrise Protea Farm,** 878-2119, where you can see the striking varieties of multicolored proteas, one of Hawaii's biggest commercial flower crops, from October through May.

Turn left onto Waipoli Road to **Poli Poli State Park**. From the road sign, it is ten very rugged, often muddy, miles to the park at the 6,200-foot level. Usually bypassed by tourists, the park has a redwood forest and other trees imported from around the world. The **Poli Poli Loop Trail** through the park is five miles long. To visit the **Tedeschi Winery**, 878-6058, turn left on Highway 370 through the town of Keokea (take the right-hand fork in the road, which has no sign) and pass the Ulupalakua Ranch. Taste their Carnellian champagne, Blanc de Noirs, or blush wine, allowing at least half an hour before 5 p.m. closing time.

On the way back to Kahului, turn right in Pukalani on Highway 365 for Makawao (or, if it's too late, save **Makawao** for Day 7 on the way back from Hana, taking the back way through Ulumalu). In Makawao, the unofficial capital of the upcountry, behind Old West wooden storefronts you'll find espresso, more and more boutiques, bagels and cream cheese, and galleries favoring local artists down Baldwin Avenue. Farther down Baldwin Avenue is the Hai Noeau Visual Arts Center on the lovely Baldwin estate. On the way down to Kahului-Wailuku, turn west from Highway 37 onto little-traveled Pulehu Road, about three miles south of Pukalani.

Where to Stay
In the upcountry, stay at a B&B near Makawao, Paia, or Kula rather than at any other accommodation. The best B&B choice in the Kula area, just a few minutes from the road up Haleakala, is beautiful **Kilohana** (378 Kamehameki Rd., Kula, HI 96790, 878-6086). The views from the charming New England-style house are spectacular,

and the hostess, Jody Baldwin, is most pleasant and helpful. Drive on Olinda Road, one of the most scenic roads
in Hawaii, five miles above Makawao to the **McKay
Country Cottage** (536 Olinda Rd., Makawao, Maui, HI
96768, 572-1453) in the midst of a 12-acre protea farm.
Stewart McKay, who is from Scotland, and his wife, Shaun,
rent a bedroom for $65 a night in their home, with its
huge stone fireplace in a living room with a cathedral
ceiling, and one of the nicest new cottages in Hawaii, also
with a fireplace.

In Kahului, the best budget choice is to stay at the
recently renovated **Maui Seaside** (mailing address: 2222
Kalakaua Ave., Ste 714, Honolulu, HI, 800-367-7000) with
nicely decorated and furnished standard to superior
rooms ranging from $55 to $68 off-season and $10 more
in season.

For sun and sand plus inexpensive accommodations,
especially in the off-season (May 15-December 1), Kihei is
an excellent alternative. In-season prices can go up as
much as $20 per night, generally with two- or three-
night minimums. The **Lihi Kai Cottages**, 2121 Lliili
Road, Kihei, HI 96753, 879-2335, are basic, homey, and
inexpensive from $54 to $59 for two persons depending
on the season, with $10 per extra person. Make reserva-
tions well in advance for these units. Tad Fuller and his
wife, Kim, are as friendly and helpful as any two
managers can be. Nearby shopping at the Kamaole Shopping Center, Dolphin Shopping Center, Azeka's Place
Shopping Center, and numerous other stores make this
one of the most convenient and economical places to
spend a few days.

From May 31 to October 31, the **Sunseeker Resort**,
551 South Kihei Road, Kihei, Maui, HI 96753, 879-1261,
has studio apartments with kitchenettes for $50 per day,
one-bedroom apartments with full kitchens for $60 per
day, and two-bedroom, two-bath apartments for $80 per
day. Rates go up $5 in season. The **Nona Lani Cottages**
(8) have full kitchens and ocean views for $60 for two
from April 16 to December. Prices go up to $79 from
December to April 16.

Where to Eat

The big, sophisticated Italian eating spot in Makawao, across from the Glassman Gallery, is **Casanova's**, $10 to $14 à la carte, delicious food.

Upcountry, **Polli's Mexican Restaurant**, 572-7808, is an excellent vegetarian Mexican restaurant with full dinners for $8 to $12. Until you get to Lihue on Kauai, you won't find better or less expensive saimin than at **Kitada's**, 572-7241, on Baldwin Avenue across from the **Makawao Steak House**, 572-8711, with outstanding dinners for $12 to $14, including salad bar. For a splurge, just northwest of Makawao, at 89 Hana Highway in Paia, **Dillon's Restaurant**, 579-9113, is a home away from home for hungry travelers with a taste for artistic cooking and drinks. Stop for breakfast en route to Hana.

Mama's Fish House, 579-9672, right on the beach in Kuau Cove about 1½ miles outside of Paia, serves fresh ono with Hana ginger and Maui onions, a perfect house salad, chilled papaya coconut soup, Mama's homemade bread, and luscious desserts, moderately expensive but worth it.

In Wailuku, across from the Happy Valley Inn, at 309 N. Market Street, **Yori's** serves Japanese, American, and especially Hawaiian food. Try squid in coconut milk.

For quick and cheap snacks in Kihei, the top chow-down choices are: **Suda's Snack Shop**, 61 South Kihei Road, and a plate lunch at **Azeka's Snack Shop**, in Azeka's Place Shopping Center. For the best bargain breakfast with the best view of Wailea, have all-you-can-eat pancakes for $2.95 on the patio of the **Makena Golf Course Restaurant** (879-1154).

For delicious splurge dinners, **Hakone's** Japanese food and environment at the Maui Prince Resort, Makena, are unsurpassed in the islands as is **La Perouse** at the Maui Inter-Continental (879-1922) for continental dining in an Oriental decor.

Itinerary Options

Instead of staying in Lahaina or Kahului, cabin space on Haleakala can be booked in advance (at least 90 days) or

camping permits obtained before 4 p.m. from Park Head-
quarters. Camping is limited to 25 campers per day in
Halua and Paliku so write ahead: Haleakala National Park,
Box 369, Makawao, HI 96768, 572-9177/9306.

Overnight horseback trips into the crater, including
cabin or camping equipment and food, start at $125 per
person. **Maui Stables** also offers half-day and full-day
trips. Contact: **Charles Aki, Jr.**, c/o Kaupo Store, Kaupo,
HI 96713, 248-8209; or **Pony Express**, P.O. Box 507,
Makawao, HI 96768, 667-2202; and for trips around
Makena and La Perouse Bay, contact **Makena Stables**,
879-0244. A half day to a full day of horseback riding,
lunch included, usually costs between $90 and $120 per
person depending on the terrain. Two-hour rides cost
between $30 and $50.

If you have good bicycle riding skills, good condition-
ing, better nerves, and the inclination to bike down from
the summit of Haleakala, **Cruiser Bob's Haleakala
Downhill**, 667-7717, offers a sunrise trip (3 a.m. departure), including continental breakfast and champagne
brunch, or an 8 a.m. departure with a continental breakfast and a picnic lunch halfway down, for about $90 per
person.

DAY 6
MAUI: HANA

Slowly snake your way to the fabled village of Hana
through a tunnel of foliage. Surprise views open from
hairpin turns, one-lane bridges, and gleaming gulches to
reveal azure water under brilliant sky and countless
streams and sparkling waterfalls flowing from Haleakala,
carving valleys for coconut, monkeypod, mango, wild
ginger, plumeria, bamboo, breadfruit, koa, and banana
trees. Isolated villages appear and then disappear just as
quickly. Trails beckon to picnic areas near swimming
holes under waterfalls.

Suggested Schedule

7:00 a.m.	Kahului-Wailuku or Kula to Paia for breakfast (last stop for gas and food).
8:00 a.m.	Drive Hana Highway with as many or as few stops as you wish.
11:30 a.m.	Arrive Hana.
12:00 noon	Stroll and/or swim at Hamoa Beach.
1:00 p.m.	Lunch in Hana or picnic at Waianapanapa State Park.
2:00 p.m.	Option: Ohe'o Gulch trip.
2:30 p.m.	Visit Helani Gardens.
4:15 p.m.	Browse in Hasegawa's General Store.
5:15 p.m.	Sunset at Hana Bay or some other viewpoint.
6:30 p.m.	Dinner in Hana and overnight.

Sightseeing Highlights
▲▲▲**The Hana Highway** (Route 36)—Acclaimed as one
of the most beautiful drives in Hawaii, paved in 1962, the
"highway" still has one-lane bridges and hairpin turns
that haven't been straightened a bit. It's only 52 miles, but
allow at least 3½ hours to zigzag at 10 to 25 miles per
hour through the 600 bumpy, twisting turns and over 50
one-lane bridges to Hana. Don't try a round-trip in one
day, but make reservations for the night and return

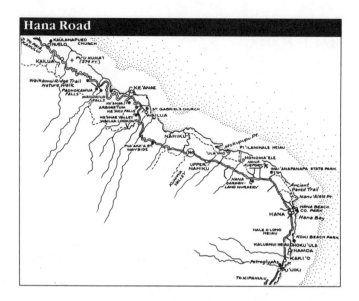

Hana Road

tomorrow. Day-trippers outnumber the local population,
so start early to get ahead of the traffic.

Stop for breakfast in quaint and weather-beaten Paia, a
former sugar town that once had over 10,000 population.
 To visit **Twin Falls** and its idyllic swimming holes, drive
about 15 minutes down the jeep trail to the double waterfall and first pool, then walk down to the others.

Pause at **Huelo's** New England-style **Kaulanapueo
Church** (1853) en route to the turnout for the nature trail
through bamboo and trees on **Waikamoi Ridge**. Campers already may have found **Kaumahina State Wayside**
and its rain forest campground overlooking the sea, and
another pool at nearby **Puohokamoa Falls**. Tucked in
the rugged coastline is the black sand beach at **Hono-
manu Bay**. **Keanae Arboretum's** tropical gardens cover
the spectrum of Hawaiian plant life: rain forest, plants,
flowers, and vegetables. Circle the peninsula to the dead
end for views of old Hawaii's farms growing taro and a
splendid view of Haleakala.

Other side roads bring you to the fishing village of
Wailua and **Wailua Lookout, Puaa Kaa State Park**,

and nearby waterfalls. A few miles away is another picturesque fishing village, Nahiku. The **Miracle Church of
Wailua** on Wailua Road at the 18-mile marker is so
named because a storm left Wailua Bay strewn with the
coral that enabled parishioners to build the church. Just
before the airport and Hana Gardenland Nursery is the
turnoff to **Piilanihale Heiau**, with 50-foot-high walls,
reputed to be Hawaii's largest. Stop again at beautiful
Waianapanapa State Park's black sand beach on
Pailoa Bay, where you can swim and snorkel on a calm
day, walk the rocky lava-strewn King's Trail past blowholes
and magnificent coastal scenery, and see **Waianapanapa
Caves**, a lava tube. Garden lovers should visit wonderful
Helani Gardens, 248-8274, open only 2 p.m. to 4 p.m.,
admission $2 adults, $1 children 6 to 16, with a tremendous variety of groomed and wild trees and plants.

▲▲▲ **Hana**—This little town remains serene and quiet.
Before celebrities like Richard Pryor, Kris Kristofferson,
and George Harrison started showing up, the most
famous resident was Queen Kaahumanu, Kamehameha's
favorite, who was responsible for the breaking of the
kapu system. Sugar was grown here from the mid-1800s
to the 1940s, when Paul Fagan, owner of a ranch on eastern Molokai, bought 14,000 acres, now the Hana Ranch,
to raise the Hereford cattle you still see today. He opened
the **Hana-Maui Resort** in 1946 (recently purchased and
renovated by Rosewood Hotels, then sold in 1989 to a
Japanese company).

Hana's main attractions, besides the cluttered, crowded
charm of **Hasegawa's General Store**, are pretty **Hamoa
Beach**, developed for guest use by the Hotel Hana Maui
but open to the public (except for the beach chairs), and
the narrow, windy 10 miles of *very* beautiful drive to
Ohe'o Gulch (Seven Sacred Pools), a Haleakala National
Park site overrun by tourists even in off-season but worth
the 2-hour round-trip drive.

The trip from Kipahulu to Kaupo or Ulupalakua Ranch
should only be attempted with four-wheel drive or on
foot. The pavement ends shortly beyond Kipahulu and

turns into a one-lane gravel road that skirts rocky cliffs
and dips steeply into gulches. (In winter, watch out for
flash floods.) The tin-roofed semighost town of Kaupo is
the start of Kaupo Gap Trail. At the end of the road is lush
Ulupalakua Ranch, and a wine-tasting tour at Tedeschi
Winery awaits (if you didn't take one during Day 5).

Where to Stay

Some of the least expensive accommodations in one of
the best locations on Maui, overlooking the ocean and
near a black sand beach, are the housekeeping cabins in
Waianapanapa State Park. For up to five nights, as
many as six people paying $10 per person can stay in
these two-room cabins supplied with bedding, towels,
dishes, cooking utensils, electricity, and even hot water.
Make reservations long in advance with the Department
of Land and Natural Resources, Division of State Parks,
P.O. Box 1049, Wailuku, Maui, HI 96793 (244-4354).

Zenzo and Fusae Nakamura's four **Aloha Cottages**
(three 2-bedrooms and a studio) at $50 to $80 for two are
the best budget accommodations in Hana (P.O. Box 205,
Hana, Maui, HI 96713, 248-8420).

Heavenly Hana Inn (P.O. Box 146, Hana, Maui, HI
96713, 248-8442) has four charming 2-bedroom and bath
units around a common area, all Japanese style, for $70
to $100, and the "little red barn" in town next to Hase-
gawa's which is very cozy and large enough for 6, also for
$70 to $100.

Where to Eat

Breakfast or a $5 plate lunch of green or fresh fruit salads
at **Tutu's** is one of the few choices for eating out in Hana.
Hana Ranch Restaurant's take-out window, lunch buffet (11 a.m.-3 p.m.), or dinner (Friday and Saturday only)
is the best value for eating and dining in town.

Itinerary Option

Red Sand Beach is truly beautiful, tucked into the side
of Hana's Ka'uki Hill but dangerous to reach. From the

community center at the end of Hauoli Road, walk around the hill on a clear, crumbly path down to the cove.

   Horseback riding on the **Hana-Kaupo Coast** can be arranged through **Oheo Riding Stables**, 248-7722; **Hauoli Lio Stables, 248-8435; Charley's Trail Rides and Pack Trips**, 248-8209; the **Hotel Hana Maui**, 248-8211; and **Adventures on Horseback**, 242-7445. Horseback riding will cost up to $150 for a one-day trip including lunch.

MAUI'S SOUTHWEST COAST AND TRIP TO MOLOKAI

On the way back from Hana, pass marvelous views over the Keanae Peninsula and visit the Keanae Arboretum to see taro fields and rain forests up close. Have an early lunch in Paia or head directly to Kihei on Highway 350 and then Kihei Road for a swim and lunch on a sunny beach such as palm-fringed Kalama Park. Drive past the southwest coast's luxury Wailea Resort to beautiful Makena Beach for the remainder of the early afternoon. Return to Maui's airport with enough time to return your rental car and catch the last flight to Molokai at 4:40 p.m. Dry west Molokai, with its outstanding beaches, is slated for huge tourist developments. East Molokai is still lush, rural, and mountainous, but with a great deal of residential construction activity. Hurry there.

Suggested Schedule

6:30 a.m.	Rise early for breakfast and check out. Head back to Paia. Stop at Uncle Harry's for some fresh banana bread.
8:30 a.m.	Visit Keanae Arboretum.
11:30 a.m.	Paia for lunch and shopping or head directly to Kihei for a snack at the beach.
1:00 p.m.	Drive past Kihei and Wailea beaches to Makena beaches. Option: If you have a four-wheel drive and snorkeling gear, head toward La Perouse Bay for snorkeling in the Ahini-Kinau Natural Reserve Area.
3:00 p.m.	Drive to the airport and return your rental car.
4:40 p.m.	Flight to Molokai.
7:00 p.m.	Check in at Molokai accommodations and dinner.
8:00 p.m.	Early to bed with an early morning ahead tomorrow.

Travel Route

Kihei is only a 15-minute drive on Routes 38 and 35 from Kahului. From Maalaea Bay to Makena, miles of some of Maui's better beaches try to lure you to stay on the island another day. Kihei beaches are the best for uninterrupted sunshine. Maalaea and Mai Poina Oe Lau beaches are best for windsurfing, Kamaole and Keawakapu for white sands, and Mokapu and Ulua for swimming. The five crescent-moon white sand beaches fronting on Wailea's resorts, especially Wailea Beach and lovely Halfway Beach, are open to the public and rarely crowded.

Uncrowded Naupaka Beach, reached from old Makena Road or through the beautifully designed Maui Prince Hotel, is perfect for swimming. Head several miles beyond Wailea to the most beautiful beach on Maui, Makena, reached by an unmarked turnoff from the newly paved Makena Road. Three quarters of a mile long, Oneuli (Big Beach) contains many tent vacationers, and Puu Plai (Little Beach), over the cinder cone, attracts nude bathers.

Sightseeing Highlights

▲▲ **Uncle Harry's Roadside Stand**—Run by Harry Mitchell and his family, the stand (adjacent to the Wailua exit from the Hana Road) sells Hawaiian food, snacks, and souvenirs with a warmth and knowledge of old Hawaii that is very rare.

▲▲ **Keanae Arboretum**—This arboretum provides insight into the cultivation of taro, traditionally Hawaii's most important food crop. The arboretum also shows banana and sugarcane cultivation. An unmarked 1-mile trail, a little tough and often muddy, can be hiked from the end of the taro.

▲▲▲ **Makena Beach**—Reached by driving down Route 31 on an asphalt road past the Maui Prince and condo complexes, the beach always is a peaceful oasis that hopefully will stay beyond the reach of resort development.

Beyond Makena Beach you need a four-wheel drive to drive to the Ahini-Kinau Reserve, where you can explore tidal pools, coral reefs, and lava flows. The reserve actu-

ally starts a mile past the last turnoff to Makena. Scuba
diving and snorkeling are outstanding in the protected
waters.

Getting to Molokai
Hawaiian Airlines, 800-367-5320, flies nonstop from
Maui to Molokai at 10:15 a.m. daily, with another direct
flight at 2:25 p.m.; and from Maui through Honolulu at
4:40 p.m, arriving at 6 p.m. Overnighters, including airfare, accommodations, and car rental should be packaged
on Maui (see "Car Rentals"). The nonstop trip takes 21
minutes (one hour and 20 minutes to two hours and 20
minutes for flights through Honolulu). Aloha Island Air
also flies to Molokai. To get to the Big Island on the morning of Day 11, leave on Hawaiian Airline's flight through
Honolulu, arriving at 9:30 p.m. Prices are lower on week-

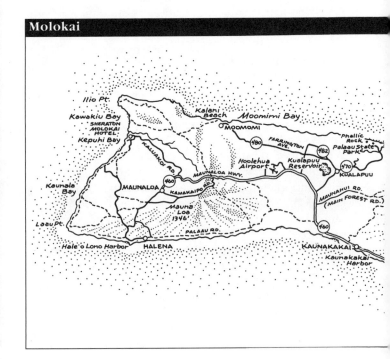

Molokai

days. From Molokai's Hoolehua Airport to Kaunakakai (by Gray Line or Roberts) is about $8, but a car rental is a must for sightseeing (other than tours).

Getting Around Molokai

Tours to Kalaupapa are available through **Rare Adventures, Ltd.** and **Damien Molokai Tours** (see p. 79), and half-day or full-day tours covering Kalaupapa Lookout, Halawa Valley, or the west end of Molokai are offered by **Gray Line Molokai**, 567-9015, and **Roberts Hawaii**, 552-2751. Molokai is so rich in ancient Hawaiian history, and so compact, that you can see much of the island for about $90 with **Native Hawaiian Tours**. Call 537-9588 before you leave Honolulu.

You can rent a car from: Tropical Rent-A-Car, 567-6118; Avis, 567-6814 or 800-331-1212; Alamo Rent-A-Car,

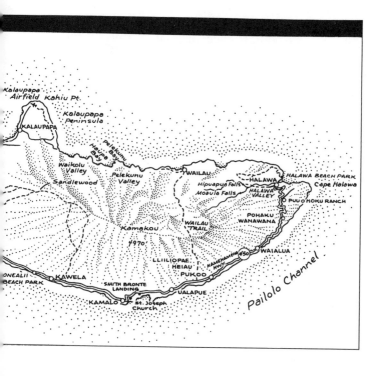

567-6188; or Dollar Rent-A-Car. Per day rates vary season-
ally from $18 for a standard shift subcompact to $24 for
an automatic compact. Fill your tank on Saturday; gas stations are closed on Sundays.

If you bring your own bike, Molokai is ideal for two-
wheeling on the east and west ends and a rough off-road
ride with excellent scenery in the northwest and southeast. Bicyclers should take the morning boat (at 7 a.m.),
the *Maui Princess*, and return the same day or preferably
a few days later by boat, with bike transportation free and
a low package rate for accommodations. Bring your own
repair kit, too; there are no repair shops.

Where to Stay
There are only three moderate-priced places to stay on
Molokai. On the ocean, the cozy newly refurbished **Pau
Hana Inn**, Box 860, Kaunakakai, HI 96748, 553-5342,
from Honolulu, 536-7545 or 800-367-8047, has rates
ranging from $45 to $69 single or double and 10 cottage
units with and without kitchenettes from $69 to $85.
Hotel Molokai, Box 546, Kaunakakai, HI 96748,
553-5347 or 800-367-8047, is a series of 55 Polynesian-
style two-story modified A-frames, each one with its
own porch and hanging bench. Some rooms are small, so
ask to see them before taking one and try to get waterfront units. There's no radio, TV, telephone, or stove, but
you'll have a refrigerator, maid service, and friendliness.
All units are studios renting from $55 to $69 standard and
$85 to $99 deluxe oceanfront, single or double. **Wavecrest
Resort Condominium**, Star Route, Kaunakakai, HI
96748, 558-8101 or 800-367-2980, on the south shore at
Ualapue, 12 miles east of Kaunakakai, on Route 450, mile
marker 13, has 43 fully equipped one- and two-bedroom
apartments fronting on a lagoon, along with a lighted
tennis court. Wavecrest has a three-night minimum, but if
there's a vacant unit, you can squeeze in for fewer nights.
The prices are $56 to $66 single or double for the one-
bedroom and $76 to $86 for up to four people for the
two-bedrooms.

The most outstanding rental unit on Molokai, near the mile 20 marker en route to Halawa Valley, is **Hale Kawai- kapu's cottage** at $80 a day double for a week (521-9202), on a beautiful private beach in a 250-acre tropical estate.

The multistory condo development is much closer to Halawa Valley but otherwise has no advantages over the other accommodations, and the buildings are not espe- cially attractive, although the units are good value.

Papohaku State Park fronting on one of Hawaii's most magnificent beaches, is the best place to camp on Molokai. **Palaau State Park** has become rundown but could be excellent if repaired. Other camping spots include **Kioea Park**, in the coconut grove, for $5 per day, with a permit from the Hawaiian Homelands Depart- ment in Hoolehua, 567-6104, and more crowded and noisy seaside camping four miles east of Kaunakakai at **O Ne Alii Park** and at **Beach Park and Wildlife Sanctu- ary**, both with county permits from County Parks and Recreation in Kaunakakai, 553-5141. To rent camping gear, contact **Molokai Fish and Dive Corporation**, 553-5926, in Kaunakakai.

Where to Eat

Meals on Molokai are getting much more expensive with- out improving in quality, maybe even going downhill in Kaunakakai.

In Kaunakakai, the **Mid-Nite Inn**, Ala Malama Street, where people used to snack while waiting for the mid- night inter-island steamer to Honolulu, has been serving low-budget meals for almost half a century. Art Kikukawa and his sons serve breakfast starting at 6 a.m. Prices for meals with small portions have increased to $7 and higher. For breakfast, or certainly along with your picnic lunch in Halawa Valley, try Molokai breads at the **Kane- mitsu Bakery,** Ala Malama Street, where the same family has been baking for 70 years. The **Pau Hana Inn Restau- rant** room serves a wide variety of dinners for around $10 to $12 (with unlimited salad bar and soup), plus a fireplace, guitar music, overhead fans, and pidgin conversation gently buzzing under the hundred-year-old banyan tree.

Elsewhere on the island, under the same hotel ownership as the Pau Hana Inn, the **Hotel Molokai** serves a tasty variety of dinners for $10 to $12 next to the water in a more attractive dining area. Shop for picnic food at the **Friendly Market** in Kaunakakai. **Jojo's Café** in Maunaloa serves everything from frankfurter and burger snacks to some of the best fish meals on the island at budget prices.

Nightlife

Nightlife revolves around the **Pau Hana Bar** courtyard with dancing under the sprawling banyan tree, a local band, torchlights at the lagoon, and local people "talking story." The bar gets a bit rowdy on the weekends. If you prefer a quiet drink and island music, try the **Holoholo Dining Room** of the **Hotel Molokai**, especially on weekends. Check the bulletin board in the center of town to see what's going on.

Itinerary Options

Whale-watching excursions run from January through April on the Seabird Cruises, Inc.'s *Spirit of Windjammer*, a 75-foot, 3-masted schooner out of Lahaina at 9:30 a.m (call 667-6834 or 800-843-8113). Or you can combine your whale watching with snorkeling around Lanai on Seabird Cruises' *Aikane III* (661-3643). Half-day trips should cost no more than $60 and with increasing competition may be as low as $30 off-season.

In winter, book a guided marine life excursion to **Ahini Kinau Natural Reserve** with Ann Fielding, author of *Hawaiian Reefs and Tidepools*. For $35, Ann, a marine biologist, provides an informal "seminar" on local reef systems and marine life, snorkeling gear, and refreshments at the Reserve, 5 miles past Wailea, where outstanding snorkeling is enjoyed by only a few of Maui's visitors.

Windsurfers will tell you that **Hookipa Beach Park**, located two miles past Paia on the Hana Highway, and the **Pailolo Channel** between Molokai and Maui are the best in the state. Contact **G & S Enterprises**, 558-8253, or **Ocean Activities Center** (879-4485 or 800-367-8047). Rentals cost about $40/day including a soft car rack.

Take more time to get to Molokai from Maui on the luxury inter-island ferry, the *Maui Princess*. The one hour and 15 minute trip departing from Lahaina's dock costs $21 each way for adults and $10.50 for children. In whale season you may see some humpbacks. Sometimes the trip can get rough, so bring along your Dramamine. Reservations are easy to get once you're on Maui. Call 553-5736.

DAY 8
MOLOKAI: KALAUPAPA

An all-day round-trip down from the 2,000-foot pali takes you to one of the most remote spots in Hawaii, the exile of lepers at Kalaupapa, where Father Damien devoted 16 years to helping about a thousand outcasts improve their tragic lives. After you return to the clifftop, take two short drives to the west and east ends for spectacular viewpoints over the cliffs, visiting Palaau State Park and possibly Waikolu Overlook.

Suggested Schedule	
7:30 a.m.	Breakfast in Kaunakakai.
8:00 a.m.	Drive past Kapuaiwa Royal Coconut Grove and Church Row on the road to Kualapuu and Kalaupapa Lookout.
8:45 a.m.	Head of mule trail for mule trip or walk down to Kalaupapa.
9:00 a.m.	Start of mule ride from Kalae to Kalaupapa and tour of Makanalua Peninsula.
12:00 noon	Picnic lunch at Kalawao Park.
3:30 p.m.	From Kalaupapa, head for Palaau State Park.
4:30 p.m.	Option: Drive from Palaau Park to Waikolu Overlook.
6:00 p.m.	Return to Kaunakakai and freshen up for dinner.
8:30 p.m.	Enjoy a quiet evening at the Hotel Molakai's cocktail lounge.

Getting to Kalaupapa
Head west from Kaunakakai on Route 460, past cornfields and the startling contrast of dead trees. Continue up Route 470 through Kualapuu to the mule trail that switchbacks 1,600 feet down to Kalaupapa.

Just a few yards before the start of the mule trail, on the west side of the road, are the stables for the mule ride to Kalaupapa. **Molokai Mule Ride**, also known as **Rare**

Adventures, Ltd. (P.O. Box 200, Kualapuu, Molokai, HI 96757, 526-0888), takes you down the 26 switchbacks on a sure-footed mule. The six-hour tour costs $85 per person. Children under 16 are not permitted in the village, and people over 225 pounds can't ride the mules. Reservations should be made at least two weeks in advance. You can also hike down to Kalaupapa and, for $30, Rare Adventures will arrange lunch and a tour of the peninsula. Hikers leave about 30 minutes ahead of the mules. A combination air/ground tour costs less than a mule trip—only $30 per person. If you fly down from Kalaupapa Airport, you'll be met by **Damien Molokai Tours** (Box 1, Kalaupapa, HI 96742, 567-6171), run by Mr. and Mrs. Richard Marks, themselves former patients. Their four-hour ground tour costs about $19 per person, daily except Sunday. For $30, they will fly you into Kalaupapa. The tour cost is extra. For all Kalaupapa tours, make reservations before arriving on Molokai! One way or another, you have to pay to go down to Kalaupapa and make a specific booking for a tour and lunch. You can't simply hike down or enter Kalaupapa unescorted.

Sightseeing Highlights

▲▲ **Kaunakakai**—This is the island's main town, which is three blocks long and, even with a few new shops, hasn't changed much since World War II and probably would like to stay that way, although the pineapple plantations have closed down, jobs are scarce, and Holokai workers commute to Maui every day on the *Maui Princess* to work at low-paying jobs. From the shoreline to the right of the former wooden wharf, you can see the stone platform that was part of King Kamehameha V's vacation home.

▲ **Kapuaiwa Royal Coconut Grove**—The grove is only a few minutes drive to the west of Kaunakakai's center. It began with 1,000 trees planted in honor of High Chief Kapuaiwa, who became King Kamehameha V. The grove has thinned out considerably since then. Beware of walking under the royal coconut palms when the wind is blowing.

▲ **Church Row**—Across Route 45 from the Coconut
Grove, a half-dozen one-room churches and a mission
school create a hive of inter-denominational activity on
Sunday morning, producing the island's only traffic jam.
▲▲▲ **Kalaupapa Leper Colony**—A few hundred yards
to the west of Kalawao Cove, this is one of the most
extraordinary locations imaginable, probably the most
isolated spot in the Hawaiian islands. A government
schooner, the *Warwick*, started transporting lepers and
suspected lepers of all ages to Kalawao Cove in 1866.
Bounty hunters rounded up anyone with any sort of skin
ailment, shipped them in cages, and dumped them over-
board near Kalawao Cove to swim to shore. In 1873, a
Belgian priest, Father Damien Joseph De Veuster, arrived
for a 16-year stay in this tragic and nightmarish dumping
ground of doomed lepers. Eleven years later, he con-
tracted leprosy himself and died in five years at the age of
49. About 60 years after Father Damien died, the dreaded
disease was finally conquered by sulfone drugs. Today
about 60 people voluntarily remain on the peninsula.
▲▲ **Palaau State Park**—Off Route 470, high on a bluff
overlooking Kalaupapa Peninsula and the ocean, a trail
leads from the parking lot up a hill through beautiful
ironwoods to the Phallic Rock, where childless women
came in hopes of receiving fertility. A second trail from
the parking lot leads to an overlook behind a wall, with a
perfect view of Kalaupapa and historical information to
explain what you're seeing.

Itinerary Options
The Waikolu Overlook—The view is well worth the
side trip on a clear day. Head west on Route 460 to mile
marker 3 to the six-mile rutted dirt road leading to the
marked Main Forest Road. After ten miles you'll pass the
pit formerly used to measure the quantities of sandal-
wood cut and carried off the surrounding mountains to
trading ships. One mile farther, past the heavily wooded
Waikolu Picnic Grove, is the Waikolu Overlook of the
valley 3,700 feet below.

MOLOKAI: HALAWA VALLEY TO WEST MOLOKAI

Drive along the south shore past mile after mile of historic sites and occasional good beaches to spectacular views of the Halawa Valley. Walk in the valley to Moaula Falls and picnic at the pool below the falls. Then, for a complete contrast, drive to the west end of Molokai to end the day watching the sunset over the island's second-best beach at the Kaluakoi Resort or from beautiful Papohaku Beach, stretching wide for about a mile along the lush coast (one day to be part of a huge resort but still open to the public).

Suggested Schedule

7:00 a.m.	Breakfast and shop for a picnic lunch in Kaunakakai.
8:00 a.m.	Start the south shore drive to Halawa Valley.
8:15 a.m.	Kalokoeli Fish Pond.
8:45 a.m.	Iliiliopae Heiau.
10:00 a.m.	Arrive at Halawa Valley Lookout.
10:15 a.m.	Drive down the valley, park, and walk to the pool at the base of Moaula Falls.
11:30 a.m.	Swim in the pool and sun on the rocks.
12:00 noon	Picnic lunch.
1:30 p.m.	Return to your car and drive to Kaluakoi Resort. (Option: from the resort, take a tour of Molokai Wildlife Park; a 3:30 p.m. tour leaves from the Kaluakoi Resort.)
5:30 p.m.	Sunset from Papohaku Beach.
6:30 p.m.	Dinner at the oceanside Paniolo Broiler.
8:00 p.m.	Return to Kaunakakai or linger for the evening at the Kaluakoi Resort.

Travel Route

Highway 45 runs from Kaunakakai along the south and east shore for 30 miles to the Halawa Valley. Virtually each mile has a historic site of greater or lesser importance, from major ancient Polynesian sites like Iliiliopae Heiau and the 58 fish ponds, to the marker where aviators Smith and Bronte landed awkwardly but unharmed in a clump of trees. Plan on a 1½ - to 2-hour drive, depending on your pace, on a road that defies haste.

The paved two-lane road twists and turns for nine miles as you ascend the green slopes to Puu O Hoku (Hill of Stars) Ranch and Lodge, dotted with French Charolais cattle. There are great views across Pailolo Channel to Maui and Mount Haleakala as you round the hairpin turn to the overlook into the four-mile-long Halawa Valley with its two magnificent waterfalls plummeting to the stream below. The paved road zigzags down the ridge in the broad, deep green valley, backed by cliffs. To the north, Lamaloa Head juts into the ocean's pounding surf. Moaula Falls is a relatively easy (except for the stream crossing) hour's hike to the far side of the valley.

Sightseeing Highlights
▲▲ **Kalokoeli Fish Pond**—Between Kaunakakai and Kawela is one of a series of ancient fish ponds along the southern shore, built in the early thirteenth century to catch fish for local chiefs and then Kamehameha and his descendants. Some are still in use.

▲▲ **Iliiliopae Heiau**—Only a ten-minute walk from the Wailau Trail sign near Pukoo, this is a major Hawaiian temple the size of a football field. To visit this site, check at your hotel desk for clearance.

▲▲▲ **Halawa Valley**—This valley is believed to be the first settlement on Molokai, dating back to the seventh century. Taro grown in the fertile valley supplied Molokai and Maui for centuries. There are two waterfalls at the end of the valley: **Moaula Falls**, an upper and lower falls with a pool at the base of the lower falls for swimming; and **Hipuapua**, a single waterfall with a pool at the base. When you reach the valley floor, a narrow dirt side road turns sharply to the left in front of the small green church to the trailhead up to Moaula Falls, while the main road runs a few hundred yards to the county park and beach.

Leave your car across from the church. Take the road for half a mile to its end, passing several houses on your left along the way. There a foot trail begins. Walk about 100 yards to a row of rocks across the trail and a stone wall and turn right down to the stream. Cross both forks of the stream *at the easiest and safest place* (you probably will have to wade across the stream). The trail goes uphill perpendicular to the stream. Look for an orange mark on a tree where the trail continues through heavy grass and mango groves (deliciously ripe from March to October) to a fork: right to the beach, or left to the lower falls following a white plastic pipe and white arrows. (You probably will have to wade across the stream.) If the stream is too broad and deep to cross, take the trail to the left near the green church, head upstream following old stone walls and a white water pipe to a fork a short distance past the Hipuapua Stream branching off Halawa Stream. The left-hand trail goes to the lower pool, the steep right-hand fork to the upper pool.

Molokai Ranch—This ranch along Highway 460 was originally the royal ranch of the Kamehamehas.

▲▲**Molokai Ranch Wildlife Park**—This park has African and Asian wildlife including giraffes, antelopes, Indian black bucks, sika deer, ostrich, ibex, sable, eland, Barbary sheep, oryx, Arabian goats, and other animals in pastureland that can be toured by calling 553-5115. A bus or van leaves on a "camera safari" four times a day (9:30 a.m., 11:30 a.m., 1:30 p.m., and 3:30 p.m.) from the Kaluakoi Resort, costing $25 for adults, $10 for children under 12. Not only can the tame animals be seen, but many come up to the bus to snack and playfully greet visitors.

▲▲**The Kaluakoi Resort**—Occupying a large part of the west end of Molokai, this resort includes the former Sheraton Molokai Hotel, Ke Nai Kai Condominiums and the Kaluakoi Golf Course. About two miles drive from the resort, farther southwest, is one of the best beaches in all of Hawaii, Papohaku, fronting on **Papohaku State Park**, the best place to camp on the island and an ideal vacation spot. The resort's low-rise wooden architecture blends nicely with the landscape.

LANAI

The silhouette of a razor-backed ridge covered with Norfolk pines stands out as your plane approaches Lanai. A profusion of great red gulches descends from the Munro Trail, which is your first destination as quickly as you can get into a four-wheel drive in Lanai City. To the southwest is a broad crescent of white sand, Hulopoe Beach on Manele Bay, your second spectacular destination. Farther to the west, where enormously high seacliffs frame the coastline, is Kaunolu Village, where some of the archipelago's most sacred ancient sites are scattered across a rocky point above the sea. The area was one of Kamehameha the Great's favorite recreation spots.

Suggested Schedule

5:30 a.m.	Breakfast at the Midnite Inn.
6:00 a.m.	Drive to the airport.
6:45 a.m.	Flight to Lanai on Aloha Island Air.
7:40 a.m.	Oshiro's Service Station picks you up at the Lanai Airport.
8:00 a.m.	Rent a four-wheel drive and buy picnic supplies in Lanai City.
8:30 a.m.	Head for Munro Trail.
11:00 a.m.	Arrive at the Hale Lookout.
12:00 noon	Drive to Manele and Hulopoe bays.
1:00 p.m.	Swim and picnic lunch at Hulopoe Bay.
2:30 p.m.	Head west to explore Kaunolu.
5:15 p.m.	Drive to the airport.
5:40 p.m.	Return to Molokai.
6:30 p.m.	Clean up at your hotel for dinner.
7:30 p.m.	A relaxing dinner and a last evening on Molokai.

Orientation

Starting in 1990, you will be able to stay at new resorts at Manele Bay and near Lanai City. (Others will be built, soon as Lanai is transformed into a tourist island.) Most

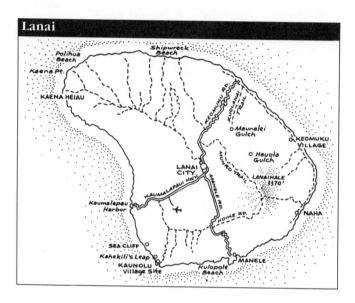

visitors come to snorkel and bask at Hulopoe Beach, per-
haps with an excursion to tiny Lanai City. They come
from Maui's Lahaina by boat for a half or full day. Very few
tourists fly from Molokai to Lanai or know that you can
fly from Lanai to Hana and Kapalua on Maui from Lanai.
Today is a round-trip, back to Molokai. Few tour opera-
tors and sales reps have even heard of the Munro Trail, an
adventure trip worth experiencing as the main purpose
of the trip or in conjunction with coastal exploration.

Getting to and around Lanai
Aloha Island Air has a flight at 6:45 a.m. from Molokai to
Lanai. The return flight leaves Lanai at 5:40 p.m. for
Molokai. The timings of the flights are excellent and the
fare is reasonable. Lanai Airport is out in the pineapple
fields, about four miles southwest of Lanai City. There's
nothing out there. Make prior arrangements for Oshiro's
Service Station to pick you up, and rent a four-wheel-
drive vehicle from them. For $4 extra, you can drop the
vehicle off at the airport for Oshiro's to pick up. With
only 22 miles of paved roads, you need a four-wheel

drive to tour the island. Oshiro's Service Station, 565-6952, and Lanai City Service, Inc., 565-6780, rent them for $75 to $85 a day.

Sightseeing Highlights

▲▲**Lanai City**—A plantation town below the mountains, Lanai City has a delightful climate because of its 1,600-foot altitude. The island's population of about 2,500, the majority Filipinos, lives in homes painted all colors of the rainbow, surrounded by colorful gardens of fruits, vegetables, and flowering shrubs and plants. The Pine Isle Market and Richards Shopping Center, next to each other on Eighth Street, can take care of your picnic needs. If you decide to spend the night, besides the two new resorts, there's one ten-unit hotel on the island, the **Hotel Lanai**, 565-6605, moderately priced, comfortable, and friendly.

▲▲▲**The Munro Trail**—This trail leads to **Lanaihale** ("The Hale"), the highest point (3,370 feet). The trail to The Hale cuts through tall eucalyptus stands, shaggy ironwoods, and Cook Island and Norfolk pines, perfect green cone shapes as far as the eye can see. Before leaving town, ASK ABOUT ROAD CONDITIONS! A recent heavy downpour can turn jeep trails into impassable quagmires. Before leaving, rent snorkeling gear at Lanai City Service for the trip to Manele Bay and Hulupoa, and pick up your picnic lunch in Lanai City. Head north 1½ miles out of Lanai City on Route 44 (Keomoku Road) toward Shipwreck Beach, turn right on the first major gravel road (marked by a sign), then turn left at the first fork and again at the next fork. The trail is 8.8 miles one way, easy for a four-wheel drive, except when it's very wet and rutted. When you arrive at the crest of The Hale, ahead of the afternoon clouds, you can see all of the Hawaiian Islands except Kauai. From the trail, head straight to Hoike Road, which connects with Manele Road and turn left for Manele Bay and Hulopoe.

▲▲**Manele Bay/Hulopoe Bay and Beach**—This bay is a splendid small boat anchorage with local and tour boats, mainly from Maui. Manele and crystal-clear Hulopoe Bay are a Marine Life Conservation District with some of the best snorkeling in the state. The palm-fringed white sands of Hulopoe Beach are picture-perfect. Six of the best camping sites in the state, with shower facilities, charge a $5 registration fee and a $5 per person fee, payable to the Koele Company, P.O. Box L, Lanai City, 565-6661.

From Maui, the best way to visit Hulopoe Beach is aboard the 50-foot *Trilogy* trimaran, which costs $125 for a full day of snorkeling, picnicking, and local sightseeing. Call 661-4743 or 800-874-2666 to book a departure from Lahaina Harbor. Three members of the Won family are crew and make the *Trilogy* one of a kind. Don't worry if you've never snorkeled before—8- to 80-year-olds learn fast at Hulopoe's tide pools and love it. Enjoy Mrs. Coon's delicious meal (on a table setting) followed by a visit to Lanai City and maybe a peek at the new 250-room resort near Hulopoe Beach.

▲▲▲ **Kaunolu**—At the end of a long dry gulch on the southwestern tip of Lanai is a fishing village surrounded by Halulu Heiau, a sacred refuge where kapu breakers sought the protection of temple priests and their gods. The village contains the remains of Kamehameha's house. Across the rocky beach, past the remains of a canoe shed, climb to the heiau site, with mortarless walls up to 30 feet high, commanding a view of the surrounding cliffs and the village. Nearby is **Kahekili's Leap**, where Kamehameha's warriors could prove their courage (voluntarily or otherwise) by leaping into the water below.

Itinerary Options
Pineapple harvesting has ended on Lanai and the island is being converted to a luxurious getaway island, with two Rockresorts thus far. The **Hotel Lanai** (565-7211) no longer is the only choice on the island. The deluxe 102-room **Lodge at Koele** (565-7300) near Lanai City has a Greg Norman and a Ted Robinson golf course. **Manele Bay** hotel overlooks Hulopoe Beach. For over $200 a night, you can have a unique hotel experience on a still rural Hawaiian island that also is a hunter's paradise.

THE BIG ISLAND: HILO

Take an early morning flight from Molokai to Hilo via Honolulu, arriving early enough to have practically a full day in Hilo. Rain or shine, the Bay City is an interesting, small tropical town that is slowly changing from a sugar port to a service economy. The capital of the world's tropical flower industry is a much better gateway to the Big Island than Kona if you wish to first experience the island's history and tropical character.

Suggested Schedule

7:00 a.m.	Early breakfast and check out of Molokai hotel.
7:55 a.m.	Flight to Hilo.
9:30 a.m.	Arrive at General Lyman Airport and rent a car.
10:30 a.m.	Check into Hilo hotel.
11:00 a.m.	Stop at the Hawaii Visitor's Bureau before exploring the town.
1:00 p.m.	Lunch.
2:00 p.m.	Visit the Lyman Mission House and Museum.
3:00 p.m.	Visit Nani Mau Gardens.
7:00 p.m.	Dinner and Hilo nightlife.

Orientation

The home of Pele, goddess of volcanoes, and the largest island in the Hawaiian chain is the newest geologically and the oldest historically. The Big Island was the first landing place of the Polynesian explorers who discovered the islands. The spirit of Polynesian daring and courage culminated here a thousand years later in Kamehameha the Great, who became Hawaii's first king.

The Big Island is amazingly diverse as a result of the volcanic activity of now-dormant Mauna Kea and active Mauna Loa and their effects on weather patterns. The

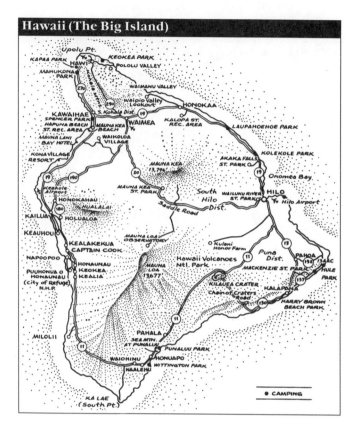

eastern Hamakua sugarcane coast is lush, indented by
gorges from Hilo to the northern tip of Kohala. The green
jungle on the east side of north Kohala turns to dry, beautiful grassland on the hilly west side down to the coast.
Volcanic rubble along the south Kohala and Kona coasts
covers the mountain slopes below tropical forests, edged
on the Kona Coast by a series of resorts, with their magnificent green expanses of golf courses, forming their
own oases in the midst of old lava flows. The southwest
end of the island turns from tropical green to volcanic
rock back to wonderful vegetation again after rounding
South Point.

Getting to the Big Island

Inter-island airlines take you in about 30 minutes to Hilo
on the east or to Kailua-Kona on the west. Fly from
Molokai on the Hawaiian Airlines flight leaving Molokai at
7:55 a.m., with a change of planes in Honolulu, departing
Honolulu at 8:55 a.m. and arriving in Hilo at 9:30 a.m.
General Lyman Field in Hilo also has inter-island jet service. Once the island's main airport, Lyman has yielded
to Kailua-Kona's Keahole Airport, which is the main landing facility on the Big Island.

Getting Around

It's a $12 cab fare for the nine-mile ride into town, and
there's no bus service.

To explore Hilo's historic sites, take a self-guided walk-
ing tour in the area between Kinoole Street, Furneaux
Lane, Kamehameha Avenue, and Waianuenue Avenue (see
Itinerary Options).

To explore outside of Hilo, Kailua-Kona, and Hawaii
Volcanoes National Park, it's best to rent a car. You can
use the Hele-On bus system to get anywhere you want to
in the Hilo Bay area or north-south to various botanical
gardens for only 75 cents, but it's time-consuming. The
intra-island buses, Mass Transportation Agency/MTA,
935-8241, are among the best transportation values in the
United States and a great way to meet interesting people.
It's only 4 hours by bus from Hilo to Kailua-Kona but
traveling by bus eliminates seeing the island's byways.
The Hele-On Bus provides cross-island service Monday
through Friday from Hilo to Kailua-Kona via Volcanoes
National Park, $6 for the cross-island run. You can hail
the bus from anywhere along the roadside. There are
daily buses from Hilo north to Honokaa and Waimea. In
Hilo, the Banyan Shuttle Bus makes two round trips (one
in the morning and one in the mid-afternoon) stopping at
most of the visitor's attractions.

When renting a car, aim for a flat weekly rental rate
with unlimited mileage. The daily rate should be around
$17.95 (winter) and $14.95 (summer), returning the car

back in Hilo seven days later. Pick your car up at or near the airport when you arrive. If you want a car in Hilo, package it with a night at the Hilo Hotel for maximum economy. Otherwise, your best choices are: Phillips's U-Drive, Hilo—935-1936, Kona— 329-1730; Robert's Hawaii Rent-A-Car, Hilo—935-2858; United Car Services, Hilo—935-2115, Kona—329-3411; Tropical Rent-A-Car, Hilo—935-3385, Kona—329-2437; Ugly Duckling, Kona—329-2113; Rent and Drive, Inc., Kona—329-3033; American International Rent-A-Car, Hilo—935-1108, Kona— 329-2926; National Rent-A-Car, Hilo—935-0891, Kona— 329-1674; Dollar Rent-A-Car, Hilo—961-6059, Kona— 329-2744 (jeeps too); Avis, Hilo—935-1290, Kona—329-1745; Hertz, Hilo—935-2896, Kona—329-3566; and Budget Rent-A-Car, Hilo—935-6878, Kona—329-8511 (jeeps, too).

Most coast roads are ideal for cycling. The Saddle Road, roads to Waimea, and Hilo to the Volcanoes National Park are hard pedaling. Bicycles rent for $3 per hour or $10 per day. Rent bicycles at Ciao Activities in Hilo (969-1717) or Kona (326-4177) or at Dave's Triathlon Shop in Kona (329-4522). An easier and fun way to see the Kona or Hamakua coast (in the dry season) is by moped from Kona Fun 'n Sun, 329-6068; Freedom Scoots, 329-2832; or Rent Scootah, 329-3250. Mopeds rent for $5 per hour, $25 per day, or $125 per week.

Sightseeing Highlights

▲▲▲ **Hilo**—Savor the seedy 1940s feel of a few square blocks of frontier-style old wooden buildings whose elegantly trimmed facades and metal roofs stream rain daily. One of the wettest cities in the world, Hilo produces luxurious flowers most of the year. Thousands of varieties of orchids and anthuriums are grown commercially and these nurseries, many clustered along Highway 11 and around Pahoa, are worth visiting. The Hawaii Visitor's Bureau, 180 Kinoole Street, Suite 104, 961-5797, is open Monday through Friday, 9 a.m. to 5 p.m.

▲▲ **Rainbow Falls**—Rainbow Drive, off Waianuenue

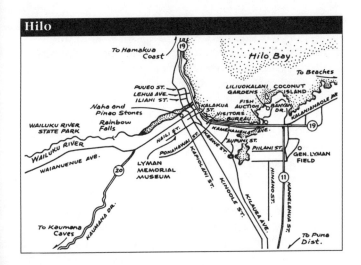

Avenue, at Wailoa River State Park, offers memorable
views around 9 to 10 a.m. when rainbows rise in the
morning mist. Up the road are the **Boiling Pots**, water
bubbling up from lava beds. Watch for the signs.

▲▲**Banyan Drive**—A drive along the waterfront is hard
to miss, since the banyan-shaded thoroughfare passes
Hilo's prime hotels. Each tree has been named for a
celebrated American, like Babe Ruth, Amelia Earhart, or
Cecil B. DeMille, as shown on plaques in front of the
trees.

▲**Liliuokalani Gardens**—Located on Waiakea Peninsula at the north end of Banyan Drive, this garden has 30
acres of colorful flowers and greenery including a Japanese garden with pagodas, lanterns, ponds, bridge, and
ceremonial teahouse. This is one of the largest such
gardens outside of Japan. The **Nihon Japanese Cultural Center**, 123 Lihiwai Street, 989-1133, overlooks
Liliuokalani Gardens and contains many authentic Japanese treasures, an art gallery, tearoom, and restaurant.
Check on special events. The gardens are always open,
and admission is free.

▲**Richardson's Beach**—On Hilo Bay's south shore is
Hilo's best beach for views of the bay and the best beach

in the area for swimming, snorkeling, surfing, and fishing. Richardson Ocean Center, 935-3830, an oceanographic museum, is located next to the beach a quarter-mile beyond the end of Kalanianaole Avenue. Admission is free. The center is open from 9 a.m. to 5 p.m.

▲▲**The Lyman Mission House and Museum** —In a restored Mission House that was built in 1839, you'll see handsome handmade koa mantels and doors, ohia wood furniture from the 1850s, portraits, and family china. As long as you don't look outside, you're in mid-nineteenth century Salem, Massachusetts. The new museum's Hawaiian and ethnic exhibits, volcanic and mineral exhibit, large Pacific shell collection, and Oriental exhibits are well worth the visit. They are open daily except Sunday, from 10 a.m. to 4 p.m. Admission fee is $3.50 for adults, $2.50 for children 12 to 18, $1.50 for children 6 to 11. Located at 276 Haili Street, 935-5021.

▲**Naha Stones**—Standing in front of the County Library on Waianuenue Avenue, this is the bigger of two stones (the other is the Pinao Stone) that in ancient days stood before the temple of Pinao near the library site. The Naha Stone was used by Hawaiians to prove the legitimacy of heirs to the Naha lineage. He who could move the stone would become king. The one who overturned it would conquer all the islands. According to legend, Kamehameha the Great overturned the stone while still a young boy. (Yes, it weighs about a ton!)

▲▲**Nani Mau Gardens**—Three miles south of Hilo, 1½ miles off Route 11 at 421 Makalika Street, 959-3541, these 20 acres grow all the varieties of trees (coffee, macadamia, and fruit), plants (orchids, ginger, and hibiscus), and unusual Hawaiian herbs and flowers that make the island famous. Also visit the Japanese garden, miniature lake, and herb garden. Open daily from 8 a.m. to 5 p.m. (with a change of ownership, the admission charge has jumped to $6 but is still worth it). An alternative is to wait until tomorrow and see the Hawaii Tropical Botanical Garden on the way north to the Hamakua Coast.

Where to Stay

The Waiakea Villas Hotel, 4000 Hualani Street, 96720, 961-2841, is half (134 units) of the former Sheraton Waiakea Hotel that closed a few years ago. It gives budget travelers one of the best deals in town: over 13 acres of tropical garden and lagoons. Very large, well-furnished rooms with private lanais overlook the gardens, and studios with king or double beds rent for $40 standard, $50 superior rooms, with king or two double beds and kitchens. The hotel has a swimming pool, a restaurant, and a great bakery (Kay's).

The **Hilo Hukilau Hotel**, 126 Banyan Way, 96720, 935-0821 or 800-367-7000, has single or double rooms, standard to deluxe, for $50 to $65. Located bayfront at the far end of Banyan Drive, they're on a side street fronting on Reed's Bay. The 139 rooms are small and plain but lanais overlook lush gardens.

Dolphin Bay Hotel, 333 Iliahi Street, 96720, 935-1466, rents rooms for $36 single to $56 twin/double and has just 18 units amid lush tropical gardens with papayas and banana trees, in a residential area across from the Wailuku River, four blocks from Hilo Bay. All units have kitchenettes, tub/showers, and no phones: budget studios, moderate one-bedrooms (can house 4), two-bedrooms (expensive for Hilo) that can accommodate 6 persons, and one- and two-bedroom apartments at $63 are available. All units have kitchen facilities. Ask about weekly rates.

The **Hilo Hotel**, 142 Kinoole Street, 96720, 961-3733, across from Kalakaua Park is as basic (and clean), with or without kitchens, as you'll find in Hawaii. Rooms have telephones. Ask for the standard ($49 per day) or deluxe ($57) room with car. Otherwise, single or double standard and deluxe rooms cost $32 and $39 for one or two persons. The Restaurant Fuji in the hotel is one of your best bets in town for an excellent Japanese meal (although for the same prices, the Nihon restaurant has much superior atmosphere).

Hawaii Naniloa Hotel, 93 Banyan Drive, 969-3333 or 800-367-5360, $70 to 80, referred to locally as the "Queen of Banyan Drive," is a high-rise right on the water, with beautiful grounds and a very attractive swimming pool area, spacious lobby, large comfortably furnished rooms, all refurbished under new ownership. For those who prefer not to stay overnight in Hilo, try **Ishigo's Inn B&B** (963-6128) in Honomu Village on the road to Akaka Falls State Park. Wake up to fresh pastries from Ishigo's bakery and head up to the park.

Where to Eat

Cafe 100, 969 Kilauea Street, 935-8683, across from Kapiolani School, is a drive-in that belongs at the top of the lunch bargain list with its teriyaki steak, mahi mahi, chicken and steak dishes, and chili. Just follow the crowds of locals. Closed Sunday. **Dick's Coffee House**, in the Hilo Shopping Center, 935-2769, at the corner of Kekuanaoa and Kilauea avenues, open 7:00 a.m. to 10:30 p.m., is unbeatable for variety and prices for all three meals, especially the specials, six days a week.

For breakfast, you can't beat **Ken's House of Pancakes**, 1730 Kamehameha Avenue, 935-8711, at the intersection of Kam Avenue and Banyan Drive. Open 24 hours, it offers pancakes all day, as well as burgers and classic roadside lunches and dinners from chicken to steak for under $8 and late-night eats and early "brunch" from midnight to 6 a.m.

Hilo has some of the best and least expensive Japanese food on U.S. soil. **K.K. Place**, 413 Kilauea Avenue, 935-5216, has cafeteria-style breakfasts and Oriental and American plate lunches and dinners at budget prices. The other K.K. restaurant, **K.K. Tei Restaurant**, 1550 Kamehameha Highway, 961-3791, offers one of the best selections you'll find in all the islands. You can get American-style dinners, but I recommend the excellent Japanese cuisine, in an Oriental garden with floor seating or regular seating. **Restaurant Fuji**, in the Hilo Hotel, 142

Kinoole Street, 961-3733, offers authentic and reasonably priced Japanese food, with outstanding hibachi-grilled food and a tempura bar, in comfortable indoor and outdoor settings. The Nihon Cultural Center's **Nihon Restaurant** (11 a.m.-2 p.m., 5- 8:30 p.m.) has full-course dinners at moderate prices and also an excellent sushi bar.

There are Chinese restaurants at two ends of the dining spectrum: **Sun Sun Lau's Chop Sui House**, 1055 Kinoole, 935-2808, is consistently selected as one of the Big Island's top Chinese restaurants, with amazingly reasonable gourmet food. **Leung's Chop Suey House**, (530 East Lanikaula Street, 935-4066, at the intersection of Kanoelehua Avenue about a mile past Banyan Drive), is in an unappealing industrial area but it serves some of the best eat-in or take-out Cantonese food in town, up to 8:30 p.m.

Roussel's, 60 Keawe Street (935-5000), is Hilo's best restaurant, a splurge serving tasty Louisiana Cajun/Creole dishes. Try the blackened fish.

Nightlife

Downtown Hilo shuts down by 9 p.m. Few bars stay open past 10 p.m. The hot spot for dancing is upstairs at **Apple Annie's**, 100 Kanoelehua Avenue. Rock'n'rollers who don't want to dance should head for **J.D.'s Banyan Broiler** on Banyan Drive after 10 p.m. until 2 a.m. For a bar where you're likely to meet interesting locals, try **Rosey's Boathouse**. There's no place to dance but an excellent guitar combo provides light background music for good conversation. Much of Hilo's nightlife centers around the hotels. For a lively evening out, the **Springwater Cafe and Bar**, Waiakea Villas Hotel, has a light menu, drinks, and entertainment from pop to Hawaiian, Wednesday through Saturday until 2 a.m. The **Ho'omalimali Bar** of the Hawaii Naniloa Hotel has a disco that stays open on Friday and Saturday nights until 3 a.m.

Itinerary Options

Historic Downtown Hilo Walking Tour: Kalakaua Park, with a bronze statue of Hawaii's last king, is next to the Hilo Hotel; down Kalakaua Street, then right to Haili Street, with three (out of the original five) churches, down Kilauea Avenue, past the Taishoji Soto Mission started by Zen Buddhists (1913), to Furneaux Lane left on Kamehameha Avenue to see some interesting architecture: Renaissance Revival (Hafa Building); Mediterranean (the Vana Building); and even Art Deco (the S. H. Kress Building). Visit Koehnen's, the best furniture store on the island, in a delightfully remodeled building at the corner of Waianuenue and Kam avenues. Turn up Waianuenue Avenue to Keawe Street, and make a left to see several wooden buildings typical of early twentieth-century Hilo, which have been remodeled.

The Saddle Road and Mauna Kea Trail: It's about a two-hour drive from Hilo's tropical nurseries to the frigid lunar landscapes of Mauna Kea and Mauna Loa where the endangered silversword plant and the nene goose, the state bird, thrive in rarified isolation. Waimea is 55 miles from Hilo via the Saddle Road, descending 3,000 feet in 15 miles from the Saddle Road through the gamebird grasslands of the Pohakuloa Area of Mauna Kea State Park. Kailua is 87 miles from Hilo on the Saddle Road, a 2 ½ - to 3-hour drive if you're in a hurry.

You can drive to the 9,400-foot level of Mauna Kea in an ordinary passenger car, though car rental agencies will refuse to rent if you say that you're going to drive on the rough Saddle Road. Twenty-seven miles from Hilo, a 9-mile spur road leads to the Mauna Kea trailhead at Kilohana (9,620 feet) and a 17-mile road up Mauna Loa. Just a few miles west of Hilo's Rainbow Falls, Waianuenue Avenue splits to the left to clearly marked Saddle Road. Cutting northwest across the island to connect with Route 190 (north 7 miles to Waimea or south 33 miles to Kailua), Saddle Road (Route 200) runs through a high valley separating Mauna Loa and Mauna Kea. Within 5 miles, you'll pass **Kaumana Caves** (on Kaumana Drive), a lava tube created by Mauna Loa's 1881 eruption. The caves contain a fern grotto. If you intend to explore the caves, bring a flashlight.

At Humuula Junction, the **Mauna Kea Road** heads north and the **Mauna Loa Road** south. On the Mauna Loa Road, if your car is tuned for high altitudes you can drive 8 miles to a locked chain across the road (weekdays), 9 miles below the observatory, or the full 17 miles on weekends past fantastic black, silvery, brown, and red-dish lava shapes to the 11,15-foot level. If you intend to get out of your car and walk around at altitudes above 4,000 feet, bring one or two layers of warm clothing (sweaters, jackets, or pullovers). At higher altitudes, tem-peratures can change suddenly to the 40s Fahrenheit and near freezing at the summits.

Four miles up Mauna Kea, there's a visitor's center called **Hale Pohaku** (House of Rock), where many scien-tists from the observatory on top of the mountain live. A private company located in Hilo, The **Mauna Kea Observatory**, 961-2634, charges a small sum for visitors to look through a small telescope at the visitor's center. It's open on Saturdays at 6:30 p.m., as well as daytime hours. Reservations must be made weeks in advance. (A sign near the visitor's center says that you need a permit from the Department of Land and Natural Resources and a four-wheel-drive vehicle.) At the stone house, the foot trail ascends northwestward, and the jeep road, the firmer and more gradual of the two, northeastward. Take one up and the other down.

Soon the terrain consists only of barren red earth covering volcanic cones across and up the mountainsides against a background of thick fluffy clouds. Hopefully Mauna Loa and the saddle are visible through the clouds. At the 12,000-foot level, a trail leads a quarter-mile from the jeep road to the **Keanakakoi** (Cave of the Adzes), where ancient Hawaiians mined stones for their adzes. Almost at the top is **Lake Waiau** (13,020 feet), the highest lake in the United States, 400 feet across and 15 feet down to an impervious bottom in a porous mountain.

The domed observatories atop Mauna Kea, sitting on snow-topped lava, have an otherworldly aspect. From Mauna Kea Observatory Complex, at the highest point in the Pacific, astronomers can see 92 percent of all the stars visible from Earth. Mauna Kea's temperature and low humidity rarely fluctuate. Today the peak houses the University of Hawaii's 88-inch telescope, two similar 24-inch telescopes, a joint Canada-France-Hawaii 142-inch telescope (with visitor's galleries open from 9:30 a.m. to 3:30 p.m. daily, and guided tours), NASA's 120-inch Infrared Telescope Facility, a 150-inch United Kingdom infrared telescope, and two submillimeter telescopes. The ancient Polynesians, too, used the slopes of Mauna Kea to get closer to the heavens: more than 20 shrines covering over a thousand acres have been discovered on the volcano's slopes.

Led by Ken and Esther Sanborn, **Hawaiian Walkways** (73-1307 Kaiminani Drive, Kailua-Kona, 325-6677) runs half-day ($45), full-day ($80), and all-inclusive 3-day/2-night hiking-camping tours ($399) on Mauna Kea and Mauna Loa, in Waipio Valley, and in the Kohala Mountains. **Island Bicycle Adventures** (560 Kapahulu Avenue, Honolulu, 800-233-2226) offers six-day ($800 includes bikes) tours from Hilo to Kona, including Hawaii Volcanoes National Park.

THE BIG ISLAND: HAMAKUA COAST TO WAIPIO VALLEY

Drive on Highway 19 along the northeast coast and stop at one of the most beautiful botanical gardens in the Hawaiian Islands. Cross deep jungle canyons in Mauna Kea's slope and drive up the steep road to Akaka Falls at Honomu. Drive along Pepeekeo Scenic Drive, then glimpse old Hawaii as you pass by tiny tin-roofed and weather-beaten plantation towns with picturesque churches to Honokaa, the macadamia nut capital of the world. Turn on to Highway 24 to the lookout over Waipio Valley. You can hike down into the valley or take a four-wheel drive or mule tour.

Suggested Schedule

7:00 a.m.	Breakfast in Hilo and checkout.
8:00 a.m.	Stop at Suisan Fish Market.
9:00 a.m.	Visit Hawaii Tropical Botanical Garden.
10:30 a.m.	Leave for Akaka Falls along the scenic drive to Onomea Bay.
11:00 a.m.	Akaka Falls State Park.
12:30 p.m.	Lunch in Honokaa, then visit the Kamaaina Woods shop and possibly the Hawaiian Holiday Macadamia Nut Factory.
1:30 p.m.	Leave Honokaa for the Waipio Valley Lookout and to explore fabulous Waipio Valley.
1:45 p.m.	Visit the Waipio Woodworks in Kukuihaele.
2:30 p.m.	Waipio Valley Lookout.
3:00 p.m.	Descend to Waipio Valley.
7:00 p.m.	Dinner and early to bed in Waipio Valley at the Waipio Hotel, or drive to Kukuihaele, Honokaa, or Kamuela.

Driving Route

The drive from Hilo to Honokaa, on a wide smooth highway following Mauna Kea's northeastern slope, is only 39 miles. Follow Route 19 and the Mamalahoa Highway, the parallel old scenic road northeast from Hilo up the rain-swept Hamakua coast, a gently rolling plateau covered with sugarcane fields ending in cliffs over the sea, dotted with tiny plantation towns like Laupahoehoe, Papaaloa, Paauilo, and Paauhau. Drive on the 4-mile Pepeekeo Scenic Drive across wooden bridges along Onomea Bay. Turn inland on Route 220 past the Honomu Plantation Store to beautiful Akaka Falls.

Don't expect to find any resorts (yet) on the Hamakua Coast, only very quiet villages holding on to portions of the old highway replaced by Highway 19. From Honokaa, a paved road, Highway 24, runs 10 miles (through—actually past—Kukuihaele) to the lookout over Waipio Valley's east rim.

Sightseeing Highlights
▲**Suisan Fish Market**—Stop in Hilo at 85 Lihiwai Street to see shop owners bidding in many languages for the day's fish catch. Arrive by 8 a.m when the bidding starts.

▲▲▲**Hawaii Tropical Botanical Garden**—Five miles north of Hilo near the start of the 4-mile scenic road along **Onomea Bay**, this garden consists of 27 acres running the gamut of Hawaii's flora, with waterfalls, streams, and a lily pond. Take a 5-minute shuttle to the gardens. The $10 adult admission fee is tax deductible; children under 16 are admitted free. The gardens are open from 8:30 a.m. to 5:30 p.m. daily.

▲**Honomu Plantation Store**—On Highway 220 on the way to Akaka Falls, this is a restored plantation store with pictures of old Hawaii. If you decide to picnic at Akaka Falls, this is the place to pick up your supplies. Otherwise, try some of the free ice-cold sugarcane and macadamia nuts.

▲▲▲**Akaka Falls State Park**—Twelve miles north of Hilo on Highway 19, then 4 miles on Highway 220 just past Honomu, is a 66-acre natural arboretum of giant torch gingers, huge philodendrons, fragrant yellow ginger, brilliant red ginger and shell ginger, tree ferns, ti plants, hapu ferns, bamboo, orchids, bananas, plumeria, many types of hibiscus, azaleas, and other flora along a lush gorge trail passing 442-foot-high Akaka Falls, one of the most beautiful in the islands. Smaller Kahuna Falls, falling 100 feet from a side canyon, makes several drops into the crystal-clear pools on the way to the main canyon below. The trail is 0.7 mile and a leisurely half-hour hike. The trail descends from the parking lot into the canyon, winding down a ridge above the deep canyon through dense tropical rain forest.

▲**Honokaa**—Forty miles north of Hilo on Highway 240, Honokaa is the second-largest city on the Big Island. This center of sugar and macadamia nut production is in trouble as the indebted Hamakua Sugar Company is forced to sell 9,000 acres of its 35,000-acre holdings to foreign investors. Honokaa remains a unique Portuguese settlement with many restored buildings and new signs of commercial life (and jumping real estate prices like the rest of Hawaii). Home of the **Hawaiian Holiday Macadamia Nut Company**, Honokaa is the place for good buys on local craft items of monkeypod, koa, red cedar, and tropical ash. Take a self-guided tour of the macadamia nut factory to learn about its history and operations.

▲▲▲**Waipio Valley**—At the Waipio Valley Lookout (at the end of route 24 just beyond Kukuihaele), a ribbon of sparkling white surf disappears around the headland in the corner of your eye as you gaze down on Waipio Valley. A mile wide at the sea, it is six miles deep in rich green, checkered with taro patches, bounded by 2,000-foot-high cliffs, and constantly watered from the pali at the rear of the valley. Hawaii's highest waterfall, Hiilawe Waterfall, cascades 1,300 feet to the valley floor. Kamehameha the Great came many times to the valley, where many great kings were buried, to renew his spiritual power.

You can hike down to the valley, or let Les Baker and the **Waipio Valley Shuttle**'s Land Rover, 775-7121, drive you down from the lookout (10 miles from Honokaa), 900 feet above the pali coast. The round-trip cost is $40 for an hour-and-a-half tour or $60 to $100 for a half- to a full-day jeep and hiking tour into the valley, including a light lunch. This same company offers the state-authorized four-wheel-drive tour of Mauna Kea, a 6-hour trip for $65 per person. An alternative to Rovers and Jeeps is provided by Peter Tobin: **Waipio Valley Wagon Tours** is a 2-hour trip by mule wagon, Wednesday through Monday for $45 per person (half price for children under 12). Call 775-9518 for reservations. Down the incredibly steep narrow road cut into the precipitous cliffside, zig-zagging down a 25-percent grade to Waipio Valley, Les will share over 20 years of fascinating knowledge about the valley. In the valley, the "road" becomes mud tracks passing through river beds to a secluded black sand beach and then on to the Hiilawe Falls. At Nanaue Falls, on the far side of the valley, are pools where you can swim. Look for an amazing variety of fruit: mountain apple, guava and strawberry guava, papaya, mango trees, grapefruit, breadfruit, and more.

If you drive a four-wheel-drive vehicle into the valley, follow the mile-long road to the valley floor to a junction of two roads: the road to the right goes to the beach and the other into the valley. The beach trail passes some homesteads along Lalakea Fishpond to the gray sand beach. The beach is covered with the thick silky leaves of naupaka. Riptides make it inadvisable to swim. Cross the valley along the beach, fording Waipio Stream. Ironwood trees (Australian Pine) front the beach. Near the north-west pali, a trail leads up the valley floor past a swampy area, soon intersecting with a second trail from the right. This is the **Waimanu Valley Trail**, a switchback trail up the northwest wall. The second trail, leading into the val-ley, follows the base of the cliff and ends at a restaurant pavilion (which never opened) on the hillside below Hiilawe Falls.

Where to Stay
As the next best thing to camping, for $15 per person per night you can stay at octogenarian taro farmer Tom Araki's

five-room **Waipio Hotel** (no water, electricity, or refrigerator, two kitchens equipped with Coleman stoves and
kerosene lamps), with reservations (no deposits) arranged
by mail at least a month in advance to Tom Araki, 25
Malana Place, Hilo, HI 96720, or contact Waipio Valley
Shuttle, or call 775-0368 or 935-7466 (Hilo). Bring your
own food from the Last Chance Store next to the shuttle's
office. It's 2 miles from the lookout to the hotel in the valley. Bring plenty of mosquito repellent for the hike or
ride. The nearby river has fresh prawns, and the road to
the beach is lined with fruit trees.

Waipio Wayside (P.O. Box 840, Honokaa, HI 96727),
Jacqueline Horne's renovated and very charming sugar
plantation home, is bordered by a white picket fence that
is unmistakable from the road. This lovely retreat has five
tastefully redecorated rooms for rent—from one with
shared bath at $45 to the Bird's-Eye Room, a $65 suite
opening onto the deck and garden. A gourmet cook, Jac-
quie's breakfasts and other meals and snacks are memorable.

The **Hamakua Hideaway**, Box 5104, Kukuihaele, HI
96727, 775-7425 (3 houses down from the Waipio Woodworks) is a B&B, less than one mile from the Waipio
Lookout, at $50 per night. Christan Hunt's two units—
the treehouse suite, nestled in a huge 100-year-old
mango tree, and the cliff house (with fireplace), on a cliff
overlooking Maui, are rustic, secluded—and excellent
value. Guided jeep trips leave from in front of the Woodworks a few doors away. Since you have to return to
Honokaa to get back on Route 19 for the drive to the Waimea Plateau, a conveniently located ultra-budget alternative for the night is the **Hotel Honokaa Club,** 775-0533,
$28 to $32. A spruced-up 80 years old, the upstairs rooms
of the 20-room club have great views of the ocean and
even TVs and small private bathrooms. Tiny rooms down-
stairs share the communal bathroom at a rock-bottom
price.

At the 2,500-foot elevation on Mauna Kea, in Ahualoa
3 miles from Honoka toward Kamuela, the rustic **Log
House B&B Inn** (P.O. Box 1495, Honokaa, 96727,

775-9990) has 5 nicely furnished bedrooms, 2 with private baths, a living room with fireplace and a library upstairs, all for $45 with an excellent breakfast. Turn left at Tex Drive-In and then right on Mamalahoa Highway.

For those who opt not to stay in Waipio Valley but to head for Waimea, very pleasant rooms are available at **Kamuela Inn**, Route 19, 885-4243, $44 to $65, with free (but skimpy) continental breakfast. The 19 rooms all have private baths, refrigerators, and cable TV. The newer, very attractively decorated and furnished **Parker Ranch Lodge** (Route 19, 885-4100, $63-$73) is a more expensive alternative, also within walking distance of the center of sightseeing, shopping, and eating. The 10 units have king or double beds, shower/tubs, telephones, and TV.

Where to Eat
On the way up to Akaka Falls, **Ishigo's Inn and General Store**, 963-6128, in Honomu Village, has munchies and a remodeled B&B. The **Hotel Honokaa Club & Restaurant**, Route 24, 775-0678, serves a mix of Japanese and American food, breakfast, lunch, and excellent seafood dinners at moderate prices. Just past the hotel is **Honokaa Pizza and Subs**. In Honokaa, believe it or not, the place in town to buy cream puffs, **Herb's Place Meals & Cocktails**, 775-7236, serves everything from Hawaiian breakfasts to won ten mein, steaks, and mahimahi.

Itinerary Options
Waimanu Valley is for the adventuresome with hiking experience and stamina. Continue from Waipio Valley for nine miles on the Waimanu Valley Trail. The trail climbs up steep cliffs to the adjoining and even wilder valley, through a series of fourteen gulches. The trail shelter is nine gulches from Waipio Valley, two-thirds of the way to Waimanu. About half the size of Waipio Valley, Waimanu is very similar. Waiilikahi Falls is about 1½ miles along the northwest pali of the valley, and the large pool of water for swimming below it is worth making your own trail there. There's water in the valley (boil or treat it, though)

and numerous beachfront campsites, or you can return that night to Waipio.

Skiing on Mauna Kea from December at least to early May is a fun alternative to baking at the Kona beaches down below. There are no lifts and a four-wheel vehicle is necessary to reach the slopes. **Ski Guides Hawaii,** P.O. Box 2020, Kamuela, 96742, 885-4188, can set you up with equipment and a shuttle to the top (jeep "ski lifts" for the day) for $96 (includes a $10 membership fee), or $136 with lodging and meals.

Waipio Ranch, operated by Sherri Hannum and Wayne Teves, has horseback rides into Waipio Valley which can be arranged 24 hours in advance through Joe Matthieu at Waipio Woodworks, 775-0958. A half-day tour costs $55, full-day $100, including a four-wheel-drive ride down and back up the valley to Kukuihaele.

Ironwood Outfitters (885-4941) at the Kohala Ranch along Highway 200 has some of the most beautiful horse-back excursions in Hawaii, matched on Mount Hualalai above Kona by **Waiono Meadows Stables** (329-0888) for $20 and $34 per person for 1- to 2-hour guided trail rides. Ascend Hualalai or Mauna Loa or follow the King's Trail along the coast of south Kona to Captain Cook's Monument with **King's Trail Rides O'Kona** out of Kealakekua (323-2388).

Route 200 from Hilo to Waimea (The Saddle Road) over the plateau between Mauna Loa and Mauna Kea, especially near sunrise and sunset, offers exceptional scenery and glimpses of wildlife. Camping is available in cabins at **Mauna Kea State Park.** Also pay a visit to the **Mauna Kea Observatory**, not as strenuous as the hike up Mauna Loa, but the scenery is just as spectacular, including the view of Maui's Haleakala Crater.

Laupahoehoe Beach Park (a mile off Route 19) is a beautiful park with lava coastline, tent camping by permit, and no swimming, please. **Kalopa State Park** (a few miles south of Honokaa) has beautiful areas for hiking and tenting with a permit. Swim in the stream flowing in the park but not in the surf.

Golfers: The fabulous golf courses on the Kona side charge very high green fees, so it would be wise to head for these east coast courses with fees under $6: Country Club Apartment Hotel, 935-7388; Hilo Municipal Course, 340 Haihai Street, 959-7711; and Hamakua Country Club, Honokaa, 775-7244.

Bicycling: The Big Island is best of all the islands for bicycling. Contact **Hawaiian Eyes Big Island Bicycle Tours** (P.O. Box 1500, Honokaa, 96727, 775-7335) to arrange for a mountain bike trip down Mauna Kea to the Hamakua Coast ($48) and then to Waipio Valley Lookout, over Saddle Road to see the island's five volcanoes ($90), through the Kohala Mountains to Hawi and Kapaau ($60), and a tour of Hawaii Volcanoes National Park ($99).

THE BIG ISLAND: KAMUELA AND NORTH KOHALA

On the way from Waipio to the base of the mountainous Kohala peninsula, travel though a temperate zone of green meadows and darker green trees to Kamuela, a village of white picket fences and gingerbread, Gothic and Victorian frame houses more New England than Hawaii. At least 50 new stores and restaurants in several new shopping centers will be open by the time you arrive,

Suggested Schedule

6:00 a.m.	If you have the energy, rise early to catch the sunrise at Waipio Valley's black sand beach. (If you stayed over in Kamuela, you can sleep in.)
8:00 a.m.	If you're not hiking from Waipio Valley to Waimanu, after breakfast return to Route 24 for the drive to Kamuela and check in. (Hikers to Waimanu, come to Kamuela tonight.)
10:00 a.m.	Visit to the Parker Ranch Visitor Center and Museum, followed by local shopping.
12:00 noon	Lunch in Kamuela.
1:30 p.m.	Leave for "end-of-the-world"—Hawi, Kapaau, and Pololu—driving on beautiful Highway 250.
2:30 p.m.	Arrive in Hawi.
3:00 p.m.	Browsing and sightseeing in Kapaau.
3:30 p.m.	Drive to the Pololu Valley Lookout and walk down to the beach. Option: Visit Mookini Luakini Heiau, Kamehameha's birthplace and/or Lapakahi State Historical Park before returning to Kamuela.
6:00 p.m.	Backtrack to Kamuela for dinner.
7:00 p.m.	Dinner, a moonlight stroll, and overnight in Kamuela.

including the Hale Kea Plantation House. One of the world's largest Hereford herds grazes on the 225,000-acre Parker Ranch.

Kamuela offers the best of both worlds as touring base: great hiking or horseback riding in the cooler mountains, some of Hawaii's most beautiful beaches only minutes away, and relatively low-priced accommodations. Leaving Kamuela, drive the 20 miles of Highway 250 between Kamuela and Hawi to visit Kamehameha's birthplace and the sacrificial temple, Mookini Luakini Heiau.

Sightseeing Highlights
▲**Parker Ranch Visitor Center and Museum**, Highway 19, Kamuela, 885-7655—Very few sailors who jumped ship made out as well as John Palmer Parker. It helps to marry the granddaughter of a Hawaiian king, as Parker did. Domesticating King Kamehameha's wild cattle, he earned a 2-acre homesite gift from Kamehameha III in 1847. The astute New Englander's descendants now have over 45,000 head on 250,000 acres extending from ocean to uplands. The exhibits and film are worth about an hour. The visitor's center and museum are open from 9:30 a.m. to 3:30 p.m. There is a small admission charge. The two-hour **Paniolo Shuttle Tour** by mini-van to Pukalani Stables, the working ranch, and the historic homes at Puuopelu costs $15 for adults, $7.50 for children under 12. Another two hours and $39 for adults and $19 for children will take you on the **Paniolo Country Tour** to the original homestead site of Mana and the Parker family cemetery, with lunch included. Call 885-7655.
▲▲**The Kamuela Museum**, junction of Routes 19 and 250, 885-4724—Founded by descendants of John Palmer Parker, this museum is a collection of Royal Hawaiiana and artifacts from around the world, such as stuffed animals and reptiles from four continents, assorted ancient weaponry, pioneer clothing, and Chinese furnishings, as well as photographs of the Parker family through the years. Admission: $2.50 for adults, $1 for children under 12.

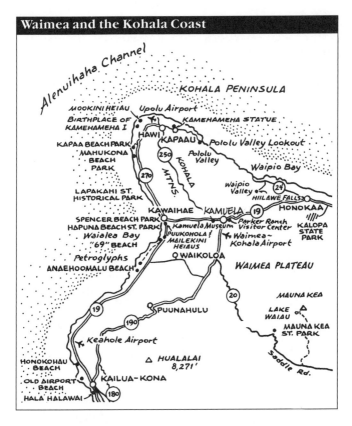

Waimea and the Kohala Coast

▲▲▲ North Kohala—This was the home of Kamehameha the Great, from which he launched a conquest of all the islands. The shores of this peninsula contain many historical sites. At the end of coastal Route 270 (Akoni Pule Highway), which passes through **Hawi** and **Kapaau**, is the steep pali overlooking **Pololu Valley**, a major taro valley of old Hawaii, accessible by a trail from the lookout.

▲▲ Route 250 (Kohala Mountain Road)—Winding through the Kohala Mountains, this very scenic route reaches an elevation of 3,500 feet. With views of the shimmering peaks of Mauna Kea, Mauna Loa, and Hualalai, and the plains and ocean below, Route 250 is a memorable drive back in time to a few settlements at the tip of the northern coast. Beyond tiny Hawi, a former sugar town with colorful old houses, and the even sleepier Kapaau, with its recent influx of boutiques and art shops, is the dirt track to **Mookini Luakini Heiau**, the sacrificial temple built over 1,500 years ago near Kamehameha's birth site.

▲ **Hawi**—This was a thriving sugar town with four movie theaters until the Kohala Sugar Company pulled out in the early 1970s. Today Hawi is experiencing a gradual revival (accompanied by ridiculous real estate prices and rents) as a spin-off from development in Kamuela and the construction of luxury ranch homes along Route 250, such as Kahala Ranch properties, one of the highest price residential subdivisions in Hawaii. Hurry to see this town and the surrounding region.

▲ **Kapaau**—The main attraction here is the gilt and bronze statue of Kamehameha in front of the courthouse, associated with another amazing story about the legendary king. Commissioned by King Kalakaua in 1878, an American sculptor, Thomas Gould, produced the heroic 9-ton sculpture that sank, with the ship transporting it to Hawaii, off Port Stanley in the Falkland Islands. With the insurance money, Gould produced another statue that stands in front of Honolulu's Judiciary Building. The original statue was salvaged by a British ship and left in a Port Stanley junkyard to be rescued by King Kalakaua and shipped to Kapaau.

▲▲ **Pololu Valley Lookout**—Just beyond Niulii, this lookout offers great views of the coastline's gorges. On your way to the lookout, you'll pass lush pandanus rain forests and Kamehameha Rock, which the mighty king reputedly carried from the sea. From the lookout, it's a 15-minute walk (which can be dangerous after rain) down to the black sand beach lined with dunes. (Don't even think about swimming here.)

▲▲▲ **Mookini Luakini Heiau and King Kamehameha's Birthplace**—You'll need some directions to find this place. Heavy rain can turn the dirt road into a quagmire. Two miles west of Hawi, at mile marker 20 on

Highway 270, take the one-lane turnoff to Upolu Airport. Drive on this paved road for 1½ miles to the end of the airport runway. Turn left on the rough, narrow dirt road paralleling the airport landing strip for 2 miles. Watch for the turnoff to the left marked "Mookini Luakini Heiau." About a thousand yards farther down the road, near a transmitter tower, King Kamehameha's birthplace is marked by a group of large boulders. According to legend, Mookini Luakini Heiau was built in a single night by 18,000 men relaying stones from Pololu Valley (where you were yesterday, 14 miles away!). Soon after his birth here, Kamehameha was taken to Waipio Valley and hidden, since omens had predicted that the child would become a "slayer of chiefs."

▲▲**Lapakahi State Historical Park**—On Highway 270, this park is a reconstructed fishing village, showing how Hawaiians lived 600 years ago. There are house plots, burial sites, fishing shrines, a family heiau, and garden plots. Open 8 a.m. to 4 p.m.

Where to Stay

The Upcountry Hideaways B&B (P.O. Box 563, Kamuela, 96743, 1-800-634-4022) consists of 3 cottages in and near Kamuela: Hawaii Country Cottage, $75; Waimea Gardens Cottage, $85; and Pau Manu Cottage, $85.

With a County permit you can stay at secluded **Keokea Beach Park**, on the side of a hill 2 miles past Kapaau toward Pololu. The beach is rocky and not good for swimming, but the bay is picturesque, with tall cliffs on all sides. There are rest rooms, showers, a pavilion, and picnic tables.

Where to Eat

It is really a pity to plan an itinerary that doesn't include lunch or dinner in Kamuela. **The Bread Depot** in the Opelo Plaza on Kawaihae Road is a wonderful bakery-deli for daily specials (Italian, Greek, who knows?), excellent French bread, soups, salads, desserts, and coffee. Open

6:30 a.m. to 5:30 p.m. except Sunday. The dining treat in Kamuela is **Merriman's**, also in Opelo Plaza, with one of the most delicious menus of fresh fish, shellfish, and meats in Hawaii. Main courses are $15 to $20 and well worth it. Call for reservations: 885-6822. Just across the road, the **Edelweiss**, Route 19, 885-6800, opened by Hans Peter Hager, a former chef of the Mauna Kea Resort, is ranked by locals among the best gourmet restaurants of the Big Island and all of the islands. Try a bratwurst and sauerkraut lunch. A cozy and outstanding interior design and the prices are reasonable. **The Parker Ranch Broiler**, Parker Ranch Center, 885-7366, serves everything from steak and chops to seafood in an attractive dining room, moderate to expensive, with a good salad bar. An odd combination of pizzas and Mexican food is offered at **Paniolo Country Inn** (885-4377).

THE BIG ISLAND: SOUTH KOHALA AND KONA COAST

Fifteen hundred years ago, the first Polynesians built a massive stone temple for sacrifices to their war god near Kamehameha's birthplace. From a reconstruction of a 600-year-old fishing village, drive to the temple where Kamehameha launched his conquest of the Hawaiian Islands. Nearby, ancient stone carvings again are a reminder of the coast's earliest inhabitants. Stop for lunch at one of Hawaii's best and most beautiful swimming beaches, Spencer Beach, with visits to at least two more white sand gems on the way south to Kailua-Kona.

Suggested Schedule

8:00 a.m.	After a leisurely breakfast, leave Kamuela for Pu'ukohola Heiau National Historic Site, then south to Kawaihae Bay and the start of south Kohala's coastal attractions and beaches.
10:00 a.m.	Visit Pu'ukohola and Mailekini Heiau.
12:00 noon	Leisurely picnic lunch on Spencer Beach or try Mauna Kea's famous buffet lunch.
1:30 p.m.	Hapuna Beach for swimming, strolling, or relaxing.
2:30 p.m.	See the Puako petroglyphs.
3:30 p.m.	Swim or snorkel at Anaehoomalu Bay.
5:00 p.m.	Drive to Kailua-Kona and check in.
7:00 p.m.	Sunset dining and then strolling near Kailua Wharf and the Hotel King Kamehameha.

Sightseeing Highlights

▲▲ **Pu'ukohola and the Mailekini Heiau**—One mile south of Kawaihae, where Route 270 turns into Route 19, is a National Historic Site (Pu'ukohola) preserving Mailekini Heiau and the John Young House. Mailekini

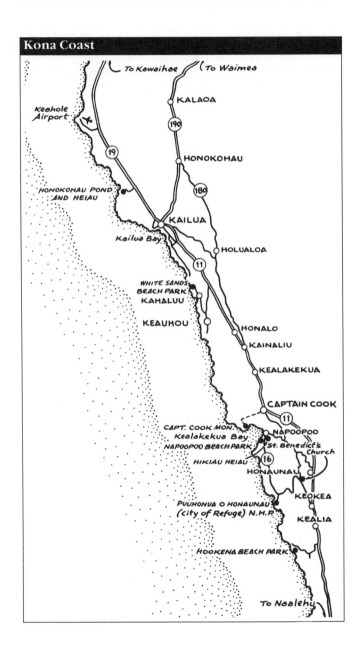

Kona Coast

To Kawaihae
To Waimea
KALAOA
190
Keahole Airport
HONOKOHAU
19
180
HONOKOHAU POND AND HEIAU
KAILUA
Kailua Bay
HOLUALOA
11
WHITE SANDS BEACH PARK
KAHALUU
KEAUHOU
HONALO
KAINALIU
KEALAKEKUA
CAPTAIN COOK
11
CAPT. COOK MON.
Kealakekua Bay
NAPOOPOO
NAPOOPOO BEACH PARK
St. Benedict's Church
HIKIAU HEIAU
16
HONAUNAU
PUUHONUA O HONAUNAU (City of Refuge) N.H.P.
KEOKEA
KEALIA
HOOKENA BEACH PARK
To Naalehu

Heiau is the last major temple built on the Big Island.
Kamehameha built this sacrificial temple in 1791 for his
war god, Ku, after a prophet told him to conquer all of
Hawaii. When it was completed, he invited his chief rival,
Keoua Kuahuula, to the dedication and slew him before
he reached shore. In the next 4 years he conquered all the
islands except Kauai. John Young, an English seaman
who became Kamehameha's close adviser, taught
Hawaiians how to use cannon and musket, converted
Mailekini Heiau into a fort, and became a Hawaiian chief.

▲▲▲**South Kohala Coast**—This coast north of Kailua-
Kona has some of the best swimming beaches anywhere
in the islands: **Spencer Beach Park**, near Kawaihae and
just below the Pu'ukohola Heiau, **Hapuna Beach** (one of
the finest white sand beaches in the hemisphere), **Anaehoomalu Beach** fronting on the Royal Waikoloan Hotel
(one of the most beautiful), and **Kaun'oa Beach**, which
fronts on the Westin Mauna Kea Hotel. All of these
beaches have public access.

▲▲**The Mauna Kea Beach Hotel**—The hotel's collection of more than 1,500 art treasures from the Pacific and
Asia is a museum in a beautiful resort set in 500 mani-
cured acres. The Robert Trent Jones Golf Course here is
the finest in Hawaii.

▲▲**Puako Petroglyphs**—Reached by the paved side
road to Puako, four miles south of Kawaihae, near the end
of which there is a parking lot and a marked trail 1 mile
long, these petroglyphs are about an hour round-trip.
The first group of carvings is only 600 feet down the trail.
All carvings are on pahoehoe lava. The origin of this rock
art is unknown.

▲▲**The Mauna Lani Bay Hotel**—With its beautiful
landscaping and gardens, in the middle of the fantastic
Francis I'i Brown Golf Course, a lovely beach and a
lagoon area, this hotel at least deserves a look.

▲▲**Anaehoomalu Bay**—The palm trees, lagoon, and
gorgeous crescent of white sand with mountains in the
background make it a popular and often crowded beach.
The bay is only 25 miles north of Kailua-Kona.

Where to Stay

No matter what you've heard, you can afford to stay somewhere on the Kona Coast.

About 30 miles before you get to Kailua-Kona, the 38 one- to three-bedroom units of the **Puako Beach Con-dominiums**, 3 Puako Beach Drive, Puako, 882-7711, start at $70 per night and will put you near Spencer, Hapuna, and Anaehoomalu beaches. **The Kona Tiki Hotel**, Alii Drive, 329-1425, has 17 refurbished units, with ceiling fans, refrigerators, some kitchenettes, and lanais for about $60 with a three-day minimum, in a garden setting with a pool by the sea, a mile south of Kailua-Kona.

In the expensive category, but still moderate compared to resort prices, the **Hotel King Kamehameha**, 75-5660 Palani Road, 329-2911 or 800-227-4700, has nicely deco-rated rooms, all with great views of the bay from lanais, starting at $85 per person.

About five miles from Disappearing Sands Beach, hid-den in Holualoa on Route 18, the **Kona Hotel**, 324-1155, may have an available $20-a-night cubbyhole with a shared bathroom. Otherwise, continue south on High-way 11 to Honalo, about seven miles from Kailua-Kona, where at 1,300 feet above sea level you have two very different low-budget choices: the very charming, Japanese-style retreat at **Teshima's Inn,** 322-9140, $25 single and $29 double; or rooms in the new wing at the **Manago Hotel**, 323-2642, may be just the south Kona bargain that you're looking for, with lanai and private bath for about $29 to $35.

Kona White Sands Apartment Hotel, Alii Drive, 329-3210, is across from Disappearing Sands Beach, the best beach on Alii Drive, with 4 units of studio and 1-bedrooms for $65 to $70, each with kitchenette. The rooms are very plain but have great ocean views and cross-ventilation. The 4-story **Kona Bay Hotel**, 75-5739 Alii Drive, 329-1393, with pool, restaurant, and bar situ-ated in the middle, has nicely furnished, large rooms with mini-kitchenettes and an appealing and relaxing atmo-sphere. It qualifies as inexpensive to moderate, $64 to $79.

The resorts of the Kona Coast, among the most beautiful in the world and appropriately expensive, include the
Westin Mauna Kea, 24 miles north of the airport near
Spencer Beach, 808-228-3000, $270 to $350 with breakfast and dinner, with one of the most perfect crescent-
shaped beaches and swimming bays in all the islands.
Also here is a very scenic and challenging golf course, a
hot-cold buffet lunch to match any resort anywhere, and
a once-a-week luau open to visitors. Another outstanding
resort is the **Mauna Lani Resort**, 17 miles north of the
airport, 800-367-2323, $275 to $365 with breakfast and
dinner. The new **Ritz-Carlton** is located at the north
end of Mauna Lani. The new **Hyatt Regency Waikoloa**
is worth a visit to see the art collection, ride the monorail
or canal boats, and enjoy the lagoon beach swimming.
Donatellos Restaurant and the Imari Japanese Restaurant
are outrageously expensive and good. The Hyatt and the
Royal Waikoloan are within the same guarded resort complex. The elegant thatched huts of the **Kona Village
Resort**, between the Waikaloa Resort and the Kailua-
Kona Airport, will no longer be so isolated as the neighboring **Four Seasons Hotel** is completed.

Where to Eat
In the budget category, try the **Kona Veranda Coffee
Shop**, Hotel King Kamehameha, 329-2911, a pleasant café
in opulent surroundings.

In the moderate price category, the **Old Kailua Can-
tina**, 75-5669 Alii Drive, 329-8226, combines one of the
best views of the bay and plentiful portions of fresh fish
dishes, like mahimahi, onion and ahi barbecued over
wood, or mahimahi deep-fried Tampico-style. Numerous
little snack shops and gourmet fast food shops are spread
around the Kona Coast. The **Oceanview Inn**, Alii Drive,
329-9998, has a tremendous variety of island and Chinese dishes for breakfast, lunch, and dinner, and special-
izes in fresh fish. Go early for dinner to avoid crowds.

Delicious Bar-B-Q ribs and chicken, the largest variety
of international beers, and a huge Sunday buffet in a fun

setting at **The Jesters Tavern**, one mile south of Kailua on Kuakini Highway, 326-7633, is the most notable recent addition to medium-priced restaurants in town.

Nightlife
Watching the sunset from the Kailua Pier is a good start. Check on schedules for local luaus if you haven't seen them on other islands. At the luau at the **King Kamehameha** on Sundays, Tuesdays, and Thursdays, you eat by torchlight at the Kamakahonu restoration. The luau at the **Kona Village Resort** on Friday nights is special. The **Kona Surf Hotel** offers a free Polynesian revue nightly and dancing in the **Puka Bar**. A good opportunity to visit the **Mauna Kea** and its **Cafe Terrace** is provided by the luau or nightly Hawaiian music. The resort's **Batik Room** features dance music. The jazz band at the bar in the **Mauna Lani Bay Hotel** provides nightly entertainment. Disco at the chrome deco **Eclipse Restaurant**, Kuakini Highway across from Foodland. For live bands in Kailua-Kona, the action is on Alii Drive at the **Spindrifter.** Even if the soft rock or jazz music doesn't satisfy you, the views of the bay will. If there's a moon to watch, take a stroll from the pier along Alii Drive.

Itinerary Options
If you decide not to take Route 25 to Kohala, there are two more direct routes to Kailua-Kona: 40 miles on **Highway 190** through the tall grass plateau occupied by the Parker Ranch to the flanks of Mount Hualalai on the Hawaii Belt Road, which becomes Palani Road as it heads for Kailua Village; or down Highway 19 to Kawaihae Harbor on the Kona Coast, a faster but much less scenic road than Highway 190. From Highway 190, take Highway 180 (which parallels Highways 19 and 11 but higher up the mountainside) and head for **Holualoa** above Kailua-Kona, a tiny, charming town that has become a remarkable art center with the **Kim Starr Gallery, Kona Arts Center, Studio 7, Holualoa Gallery,** and others. Then, instead of descending to touristy Kona right away, check

in at the delightful, attractive **Holualoa Inn B&B** (P.O. Box 222, Holualoa, Kona, 96725, 324-1121) on the slopes of Mt. Hualalai. From the rooftop gazebo, enjoy views of the countryside which match any on the Big Island, especially at sunset. The price to stay at the mansion on this 40-acre estate is high, $85 to $125 single and double.

Scuba and skin-diving off the Kona Coast are outstanding from north Kona's **Spencer Beach, Hapuna Beach**, and **69 Beach** to **Napoopoo Beach, Pu'uhonua O Honaunau Park**, and **Hookena Beach** in south Kona. The water is very clear and flat, protected from trade winds by Mauna Kea and Mauna Loa. The lava rock reefscapes are home to colorful red pencil urchins, moorish idols, lionfish, butterfly angelfish, green and yellow trumpetfish, and spotted moray eels. At the **Old Airport Beach**, nudibranchs, cowries, puffers, and scorpionfish hide in the coral heads. If you are a veteran snorkeler or ready to learn, don't miss **Kealakekua Underwater State Park**'s marine preserve, with its myriad tropical fish and spectacular coral growths. Skin-diving and scuba diving also are excellent at **Hale Halawai, Kahaluu Beach Park**, and **Napoopoo Beach Park** in South Kona. **Honokohau**, two miles north of Kailua, better known for nude sunbathing, has snorkeling, too (stay out of the shark-frequented harbor). For cruises out to the best snorkeling and diving reefs off the Kona Coast, contact: **Kamanu Charters**, 329-2021; the **Gold Coast Divers** in the King Kamehameha Hotel, 329-1328; **Dive Makai**, 329-2025; **Jack's Diving Locker**, 329-7585; **Scuba Schools of Kona**, Honokohau Harbor, 329-2661; **Fair Wind** (322-2788); or **Sea Paradise Scuba** (322-2500). You can rent equipment and take instruction from most of these same companies. A morning snorkel or dive cruise, with equipment, starts at $45 adults.

Marlin fishing and other game fishing off the Kona Coast is reputedly the finest in the world. Charters operating out of Kailua-Kona usually charge $350 for a full eight- to nine-hour day or $85 per person for a half day, four to five hours. Reserve your charter as far ahead as possible, paying a 25 percent deposit. Contact: **Kona Coast Activities,** 329-2971; **Pamela Big Game Fishing,** 329-1525; **Roy Gay,** 329-6041; **Kona Charter Skippers' Association**, 329-3600; **Twin Charter Sportfishing**, 329-4753; **Seawife Charters,** 329-1806; **Lucky Lil Sportfishing**, 325-5438; **Aloha Charter Fishing and Activities**, 329-2200; **Omega Sport Fishing,** 325-7859; or **Marlin Country Charters,** 326-1666.

Dinner Cruise: Capt. Beans' Cruises (329-6411) departs daily from Kailua-Kona Pier at 5:15 p.m. for a 2 ½ -hour sunset cruise, all-you-can-eat buffet, dance, and other music, adults only $42.

Golfers: At the magnificent and celebrated courses of · the Kona resorts, Mauna Kea Beach, Mauna Lani Resort, Waikoloa Beach Gold Club Course, Sea Mountain, and Keauhou Kona, the greens fees for nonguests are up to $125.

THE BIG ISLAND: KONA COAST

Explore the sun-soaked region of jagged lava fields and tropical waters around the Kona Coast's major resort town, Kailua-Kona. You'll understand why Kamehameha spent the last 7 years of his life beside Kailua Bay. Robert Louis Stevenson saw Kailua Village as "the sleepiest, quietest, Sundayest looking place you can imagine." The town is becoming very commercial very fast and losing charm but still is enjoyable for shopping and historic sights along Alii Drive. Driving down the Kona Coast to the remarkably clear waters of Kealakekua Bay is the best part of the day.

Suggested Schedule

8:30 a.m.	Leisurely breakfast.
9:30 a.m.	Walking tour of Kailua-Kona including the Hotel King Kamehameha, Kailua Pier, Hulihee Palace, and Mokuaikaua Church.
12:00 noon	Picnic lunch at Magic Sands Beach or lunch at Teshima's Restaurant in Honalo.
1:00 p.m.	Visit the Royal Kona Coffee Mill and Museum.
2:00 p.m.	On the shores of beautiful Kealakekua Bay, pay a homage visit to the Captain Cook Monument.
3:00 p.m.	Pu'uhonua O Honaunau Park in the City of Refuge National Historical Park.
4:30 p.m.	Visit St. Benedict's Church, Kona's famous "painted church."
6:00 p.m.	Watch the sunset from Hale Halawai Park in Kailua before dinner and socializing.

Orientation

As you enter Kailua-Kona, Highway 19 becomes Highway 11 a few miles south of the intersection with Palani Road (Highway 190). Palani Road passes two shopping centers before crossing Kuakini Highway to become Alii Drive.

Directly ahead on the right, as Alii Drive curves past
Kailua Pier, is the Hotel King Kamehameha. Glass-bottom
boat rides, fishing charters, and lunch and dinner cruises
sail from the pier into the crystal blue waters of Kailua
Bay. Kamakahonu Beach and the lagoon extending from
the hotel were the home of King Kamehameha the Great
before he died in 1819 and the site of the Ahuena Heiau,
now being restored. South of the pier along Alii Drive,
the Hulihee Palace and Museum is on the bay side now,
and across the street is the 112-foot steeple of Mokuaikaua Church. St. Michael's Church is another 2 miles
south, beyond the intersection of Hualalai Road (Route
182) with Alii Drive and Highway 19. Now get in your car
and drive south on Alii Drive to Magic Sands Beach for a
picnic lunch. And from there take Kam III Road to Highway 11 through the small villages of Honalo, Kainaliu, and
Kealakekua, turning to Kealakekua Bay on Napoopoo
Road for about 3 miles to Middle Keli Road. Turn right to
the Royal Kona Coffee Mill and Museum. From near the
mill, follow the winding road down to Kealakekua Bay,
where you can see the Captain Cook Monument, a white
obelisk at the north base of the cliffs. A rough, unmarked
one-lane road continues south through lava fields to
Pu'uhonua O Honaunau (City of Refuge) National Historic
Park, 29 miles south of Kailua-Kona on Highway 160.
Nearby is Keei Beach, a secluded gem with wonderful
views of Kealakekua Bay.

Follow Highway 160 back to Highway 11, and watch for
a turnoff to the left (Highway 16 near Keokea) for St.
Benedict's Painted Church.

Sightseeing Highlights

▲▲▲ **King Kamehameha's Royal Palace**—The
restored palace grounds adjacent to the Hotel King Kamehameha include **Ahuena Heiau**, a lava rock platform
with thatched buildings and wooden gods on its own
small island adjacent to the shore and connected by a
footbridge. Free guided tours of the displays and royal
grounds are offered Monday through Friday at 1:30 p.m.

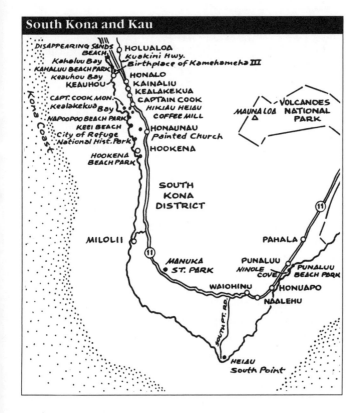

South Kona and Kau

▲▲ Hulihee Palace—A gracious two-story building stands in the middle of town just down Alii Drive from the King Kamehameha Hotel. It was used in the 1880s by King David Kalakaua as a summer palace. Restored to its former elegance, it features nineteenth-century furnishings and artifacts. The hours are 9 a.m. to 4 p.m. with a $4 admission fee.

▲ Mokuaikaua Church—Directly across Alii Drive from the Hulihee Palace, this is the oldest church in the islands. Completed in 1837, 17 years after the first missionaries arrived, the lava and coral structure with the white steeple is a local landmark.

▲ The Royal Kona Coffee Mill—On Napoopoo Road near the town of Captain Cook, this mill has been grinding and roasting Kona coffee for nearly a century. The coffee trees are grown on just a few thousand acres, spread over 600 farms between 700 and 2,000 feet, with perfect temperature and soil. The highlight of the visit is the collection of old photographs showing harvests in the days when "Kona nightingales" (mules) carried the coffee beans to the mill.

▲ **Hikiau Heiau**—In Kealakekua Bay is a reconstruction of the temple where Captain Cook was killed in 1779. The Captain Cook Monument rises across the bay.

▲▲▲ **Pu'uhonua O Honaunau National Historic Park** (Visitor's Center, 328-2326)—One of the few places where kapu violators traditionally could take refuge was here. Once inside the huge lava barricade, after swimming through shark infested waters and scaling a 10-foot wall, they were safe from their pursuers. The compound is surrounded by tall royal palms and bordered by a wall 1,000 feet long, 10 feet high, and 17 feet wide, laid without mortar. See Hale O Keawe Heiau, a sixteenth-century temple reconstructed with traditional tools and techniques by local craftsmen. Wooden gods that faced the seas centuries ago stand there once more. Techniques of canoe carving, weaving, and other early Hawaiian crafts are demonstrated around the park. Keoneele Cove is an excellent place to picnic next to tidepools. The admission is free, and it's open daily from 7:30 a.m. to 5:30 p.m. Rangers give tours from 10 a.m. to 3:30 p.m.

▲▲ **St. Benedict's Painted Church**—On Highway 160 (heading up to Highway 11), this church was decorated inside in the early 1900s by Father John Berchmans Velghe, a Belgian priest. The walls, ceiling, and pillars bear copies of medieval religious works and six Biblical scenes with Hawaiian motifs, for the benefit of parishioners who couldn't read. From here Volcanoes National Park is about 100 miles, a 3-hour drive that is better left for tomorrow.

Where to Eat

Teshima's, Highway 11, Honalo, 322-9140, 7 miles south of Kailua-Kona, has been open continuously since 1943.

When Mrs. Teshima guides you to your table and offers complimentary sake, you know that this off-the-beaten-track restaurant is special. Have a teishoku combination tray lunch with miso soup, ahi sashimi, crisp shrimp, and vegetable tempura any day of the week. Reasonable prices and large portions of delicious beef sukiyaki and Portuguese sausage make this local restaurant a must. For more conventional American fare, try **Poki's** (329-3195), next to Magic Sands Beach, serving lunches from 11:30 to 2:30 in pleasant surroundings.

Itinerary Options
Instead of returning to Kailua-Kona, continue south on Highway 11 to mile marker 77. Shortly thereafter, turn left on Donala Street to **South Point Bed & Breakfast** (Hei 92-1408 Donala Drive, Captain Cook, 96704, 929-7466), midway between Kona and Volcano. Singles and doubles are $55 per night. South Point (**Ka Lae**), site of the first Polynesian landings on the islands and the southernmost point in the United States, is a windswept cape of parched earth and blooming wildflowers, with windmills, the remains of Kalalea Heiau, a fishermen's shrine, and fishermen's boats moored to the cliffside. Hawaiians once moored their canoes here on rings cut into the edges of lava flow. South Point is 12 miles from Highway 11. **Green Sand Beach,** consisting of olivine crystals, is located 5 miles east of South Point, accessible only on foot or by four-wheel drive, down a very tricky trail to a beach unsafe for swimming. There is golf nearby at **Discovery Bay** and **Sea Mountain**.

THE BIG ISLAND: SOUTH KONA TO HAWAII VOLCANOES NATIONAL PARK

The fire goddess, Pele, chose Mauna Loa and Kilauea to show the world her powers. Today the two volcanoes comprise Hawaii Volcanoes National Park. Plan ahead and make reservations at the Kilauea Lodge for a two-night stay in the park.

Suggested Schedule

7:00 a.m.	Breakfast, check out of Kailua and an early drive to Hawaii Volcanoes National Park.
8:30 a.m.	Visit Milolii.
9:30 a.m.	Manuka State Park.
10:00 a.m.	Optional South Point side trip.
10:45 a.m.	Punaluu Beach.
12:00 noon	Check in at the Kilauea Lodge.
12:30 p.m.	Lunch.
1:30 p.m.	Kilauea Visitor's Center.
2:15 p.m.	Crater Rim Road tour to Thurston Lava Tube, Devastation Trail, and Halemaumau Trail.
4:00 p.m.	Drive Chain of Craters Road to visit Puu Huluhulu.
6:30 p.m.	Dine at the Kilauea Lodge.

Driving Route

The 53-mile drive from Kailua-Kona to South Point (Ka Lae) past Honaunau is covered with vegetation except for patches or swaths of lava flow. Past Hookena, whose gray sand beach is the best in south Kona for swimming and body surfing, Highway 11 crosses the 1919, 1936, and 1950 Mauna Loa lava flows and passes a huge macadamia nut orchard. A narrow, winding, bumpy, six-mile spur road through lava flows leads down to Milolii, a Hawaiian-Filipino fishing community about 2,000 feet below the highway.

The next stopping place, 41 miles from Kailua, is the Manuka State Park. From there, the Belt Road follows the old Mamalahoa Trail 12 miles to the turnoff to South Point Road and the southernmost point in the United States. It's another 12 miles through flat treeless terrain, down a narrow paved road, to the desolate spot where Polynesians may have landed as early as A.D. 150. Fishermen still brave the currents and winds in tiny boats for the plentiful tuna and ahi. Through Waiohinu, Naalehu, and Ninole, it's only a short side trip to Punaluu Beach Park's black sand beach. Beyond Pahala's Ka'u Sugar Mill and its tall smokestack, the countryside turns to rolling green hills and sugarcane fields, macadamia nut orchards and beautiful valleys with ohia forests. After you pass the Volcano Golf Course, you'll approach Hawaii Volcanoes National Park.

Proceed to the marked turnoff from Highway 11 to the Kilauea Visitor's Center. If you're staying tonight at the Volcano House, across the road from the center, check in now.

Drive clockwise around the 11-mile Crater Rim Road that starts near the Visitor's Center. Stop at the 400-foot-long Thurston Lava Tube, reached by a short walk through a fern trail, and at Devastation Trail. Then drive 4 miles down the Chain of Craters Road to the Mauna Ulu parking lot, for a walk to Puu Huluhulu.

Sightseeing Highlights
▲▲**Milolii**—Five miles off Route 11 south of Kailua, this is an authentic South Seas fishing village with marvelous tidepools. Built on lava rubble, this active fishing village's houses of old lumber and corrugated iron are a relic of a past era. Outrigger canoes are powered by outboards, but the method of fishing for opelu, a type of mackerel, hasn't changed.
▲**Manuka State Park**—On Route 11 south of Milolii is a lovely botanic park several thousand feet above the ocean.
▲▲**Punaluu Beach Park**—One mile off Route 11 north of Naalehu (the "southernmost town in the U.S.A.") is a beautiful black sand beach in a palm-fringed lagoon set-

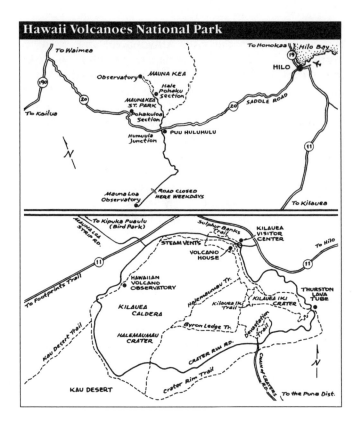

Hawaii Volcanoes National Park

ting, with a visitor center, a museum, and nearby **Sea Mountain** resort with the **Punaluu Black Sands Restaurant** overlooking the beach. Camping is allowed with a permit. To escape tourist crowds, head about one-third mile south to **Ninole Cove** for more privacy. On the hill above the beach is a tiny church with a shrine in its graveyard to Henry Opukahaia, the Punaluu boy who sailed to America in 1809 and persuaded Christian missionaries to come to save the souls of his people.

▲▲▲**Hawaii Volcanoes National Park**—Two active volcanoes are here: Mauna Loa, 13,677 feet high and the most massive mountain on earth, and Kilauea Caldera, 4,000 feet, tucked into Mauna Loa's side and encircled by the 11-mile Crater Rim Drive. Kilauea's accessibility has earned it the nickname of the "drive-in volcano." Kilauea erupts about every 10 months. (If it erupts while you're in the vicinity, watch out for the tour buses rather than the lava flow.) Mauna Loa has erupted in fiery fountains, but relatively quietly, once every 3 or 4 years. In 1984, for the first time in 103 years, both volcanoes erupted simultaneously. For 22 days, lava spewed from a vent near the Northeast Rift and Red Hill to within a few miles of Hilo.

The 344-square-mile park has three entrances on the flanks of Mauna Loa: the east entrance, from Highway 11, 30 miles directly southwest of Hilo; the southeast entrance via Highway 130, branching off Highway 11 south of Hilo, heading south through the Puna District, connecting with Chain of Craters Road through the park's Kalapana Section (this is the way you will leave the park day after tomorrow); and the southwest entrance on Highway 11 at the Kilauea Visitor's Center, which is the best way to enter the park. During my last visit (November 1990) shifts were under way in the 6½-year-old Kilauea eruption. After more than 3 years of stable lava flows from the vent to the ocean near Kupapau Point, the flows were taking new paths, tossing lava all around lower Puna, flowing over Kaimu Black Sand Beach, filling Kaimu Bay, and wiping out the Kalapana subdivision. Ranger residences recently were destroyed. Pele is restless.

▲▲▲**Crater Rim Drive**—Circling the Kilauea Crater, this drive passes through 11 miles of rain forest, desert, lava flows, and pumice piles. You'll see two types of lava: smooth-looking ropy lava called pahoehoe and, lower down the slope, the rough cindery type known as aa.

▲▲**Thurston Lava Tube**—A short trail through the most accessible lava tunnel (450 feet long and 10 feet high), this lava tube is enclosed at the entrance and exit by a fern jungle.

▲▲**Devastation Trail**—This half-mile elevated boardwalk crosses a desolate black lava field through a skeletal forest of ohia tree trunks entombed during the 1959 eruption of Kilauea Iki (Little Kilauea). Gradually returning to life, the trees sprout unusual aerial roots.

▲▲▲**Halemaumau Trail**—This trail can be entered
from 2 locations: next to the Visitor's Center, for a 6-mile,
5-hour round trip; or from the opposite side of Crater
Rim Drive, where it's only a quarter-mile down. Today
the shorter walk fits in better.

▲▲▲**Chain of Craters Road**—This road is a 27-mile
drive from Kilauea Visitor's Center to the 4,000-foot
mark above the coast. The old highway was covered by
lava and cinders from Mauna Ulu, a "growing" volcano
that can be seen best from the top of Puu Huluhulu, an
old crater. (The road may be closed to traffic to Routes
130 and 137 through the Puna District because of lava
flows. Check at the Kilauea Visitor's Center for an adjust-
ment of Day 18's itinerary.)

Where to Stay
Three B&Bs secluded in Volcano Village provide the best
variety of B&B choices in one place in all Hawaii. **My
Island B&B** (P.O. Box 100, Volcano, 96785, 967-7216) is
a historic 100-year-old home sitting in a marvelous tropical garden. Rates range from $30 shared bath to $55 private studio with bath. **Volcano B&B** (Konelehua and
Wright roads in Volcano, 967-7779) has 3 rooms with
shared bath, 2 up and 1 down, that range from $45 to $55
depending on season and number in the party. **Kilauea
Lodge** (and restaurant, see below; P.O. Box 116, Volcano
Village, 96785, 967-7366), located one mile (Hilo-side)
from Volcanoes National Park, offers uniquely decorated
rooms with fireplaces, private baths, and the best B&B
breakfast on the Big Island, from $75. It was built in 1938
as a YMCA camping and lodging facility, and recently
Albert and Lorna Jeyte remodeled the lodge and restaurant. Seven new rooms will be added (in a new complex)
to the 4 existing rooms of one of the best B&Bs in Hawaii.

Carson's Volcano Cottages have some of the coziest
cottages in one of the loveliest landscaped settings on the
Big Island. After a day at the volcano and some time in
their hot tub under the stars, you feel at peace with the
world. Rates are only $50 to $65 for two. Contact Tom
Carson, P.O. Box 503, Volcano, HI 96785, 967-7683.

Namakini Palo Campground behind the Hawaii Volcano Observatory requires a permit from Park Headquarters to camp free for up to 7 days. Cabins can be rented through Volcano House for $24 single or double, including sheets, pillows, towel, soap, and blanket. **Kipuka Nene**, 10 miles south of Park Headquarters, also requires a permit and is free. The **Niaulani Cabin**, rented by the Division of State Parks, Hilo, on Old Volcano Road about a half-mile from the Volcano General Store, costs from $10 for a single person to $60 for six people.

There are two very different places to stay along Route 11 en route to the park: ultra-budget **Shirakawa Hotel-Motel**, 929-7462 in Waiohinu, with kitchenettes ($30) and rooms without cooking, $22 single, $25 double; and the **Sea Mountain** at Punaluu, 928-8301, deluxe condos, studio $75 to 2-bedroom $120, with a golf course and a restaurant, located between a volcanic headland and a beautiful black sand beach, all surrounded by surprisingly lush Kau District vegetation from the coast up Mauna Loa.

Where to Eat
Right at the beach, the **Punaluu Black Sands Restaurant**, 928-8528, has lunches and dinners at moderate to expensive prices. Pick up a take-out snack lunch to eat in the picnic area at Bird Park Trail. The nearby **Sea Mountain Golf Course & Lounge**, Punaluu, 928-6222, serves a simple breakfast and lunch and dinner with excellent views of the volcanoes over the golf course.

About 2 miles from the park in Volcano Village, you have three choices. The gourmet **Lodge Restaurant**, 967-7366 (try the seafood Mauna Kea or the Fettuccini Primavera, with Kilauea Lodge coffee for dessert and Sunday Surprise at the marvelous Sunday brunch), 10:30 a.m. to 2:30 p.m., closed for lunch in off-season. Reservations essential. **Volcano House Restaurant**, 967-7321, offers moderate-to-expensive breakfast, buffet lunch, or dinner with fantastic views on the rim of Kilauea Crater looking out on lava and steam.

Through the Puna District there's only the **Kalapana Drive-In**, Route 13, across from the "Painted Church," 965-9242, for budget breakfast and lunch.

Itinerary Options
If you have extra time, hike in the Hawaii Volcanoes National Park on the **Crater Rim Trail**, a strenuous full-day 11.6-mile trail that begins in front of Volcano House and circles **Kilauea Crater**, passing the **Kau Desert**, the Southwest Rift area, and a fern forest. Hike counterclockwise to get through the Kau Desert before the noontime sun. The well-marked trail crosses Crater Rim Road several times and passes all of the sightseeing attractions that you see on the drive. Bring warm clothing, a snack lunch, and water.

If you have extra time, **Halemaumau Trail** (3.1 miles one way) starts at Park Headquarters, descends into Kilauea Caldera, and crosses the crater floor. It affords fantastic views into steaming Halemaumau Crater, then climbs to join the Crater Rim Trail.

Even with very little time, be sure to take the **"Earthquake Trail,"** a 0.6-mile round-trip along the broken roadway of Crater Rim Drive, hit by a 6.6 earthquake in 1983. Walk on the broken roadway to **Waldron Ledge** to peer into the Kilauea Caldera and visualize the power of volcano and earthquake in this area.

HAWAII VOLCANOES NATIONAL PARK

Mauna Loa Road takes you up to a nature sanctuary, an ideal picnic spot. A lookout at 6,700 feet up Mauna Loa provides panoramic views of the park. Return to Highway 11 and head south for a trek across a section of the Kau Desert to see 200-year-old footprints of ill-fated warriors who died in their tracks challenging Kamehameha's war god, Kukailmoku. One of Hawaii's best collections of local arts and crafts awaits at the Volcano Art Center.

Suggested Schedule

9:00 a.m.	See film about park geology and volcanic activity at the Visitor's Center and take a self-guided tour in the museum.
10:00 a.m.	Sulphur Banks and Steam Vents walk.
10:30 a.m.	Mauna Loa Road to Bird Park.
11:30 a.m.	Picnic lunch in Bird Park.
12:30 p.m.	Continue up Mauna Loa Road to Overlook.
1:30 p.m.	Descend to Kau Desert Footprints Trail.
2:00 p.m.	Walk Kau Desert Footprints Trail or the Kilauea Iki Trail.
3:00 p.m.	Return to Volcano House for some refreshments (and possibly to your accommodations for cleanup and a change of clothing).
4:00 p.m.	Browse at the Volcano Art Center.
6:00 p.m.	Early dinner and turn in early after enjoying the Volcano House's fireplace.

Sightseeing Highlights

▲▲▲ **Kilauea Visitor's Center**—Best seen early in the morning before hordes of visitors arrive, the free film shows highlights of past eruptions. See the flora and fauna exhibits and get up-to-date hiking information from the park rangers.

▲ **Sulphur Banks**—Here, Kilauea releases water into cracks or fumaroles to rise as sulphur gases. The nearby Steam Vents don't contain the sulphur.

▲▲ **Halemaumau Crater**—Just past the Hawaiian Volcano Observatory, this crater steams and shows its latent power. Along the trail a series of plaques tells about the area's geology and history.

▲▲ **Mauna Loa Road**—Follow Highway 11 past the Sulphur Banks and the Volcano Golf Course (away from the volcano center) to the Mauna Loa Strip Road. This road takes you up to **Kipuka Puaulu** (Bird Park), an oasis created when the Mauna Loa lava flow divided and left about 100 acres of native plants untouched. The park contains picnic grounds, exhibits about the park's plants and birds, a mile-long nature trail among some of the world's rarest plants, and a bird sanctuary. Continue along the 10-mile paved road up to the 6,682-foot level to a parking area and lookout. The road then climbs 18.3 miles to the south rim of Moku'aweoweo Caldera at 13,250 feet. If you want to hike the strenuous trail to the summit, obtain a Trail Guide and backcountry permit at the Visitor's Center.

▲▲ **The Kau Desert Footprints Trail**—This trail is on Route 11 about four miles south of the Mauna Loa Road. The 1.6-mile round-trip leads across desolate pahoehoe and aa to where about 80 warriors were crossing the desert to battle Kamehameha's warriors when Kilauea erupted. Toxic gases engulfed them and killed them in their tracks. This incredible event was seen as a sign from the gods, endorsing Kamehameha.

▲ **Volcano Art Center**—This art center, housed in the original Volcano House, sells local paintings, handicrafts, and jewelry from 8:30 a.m. to 5 p.m. The selection is the best on the island for Big Island art.

Itinerary Options
Kilauea Iki Trail is 3 miles long, takes about 3 hours, and is moderately strenuous. This volcano is remem-

bered for its 1959 eruption, which caused a 2,000-foot
fountain of fireworks for 36 days, creating the area
through which Devastation Trail passes. From Park Headquarters, drive south (left) 1.5 miles on Crater Rim Road
to the **Kilauea Iki Overlook**. Park and find the trail
entrance at the north end of the parking lot. Walk counterclockwise, through a forest of tree ferns, to the junction with the **Byron Ledge Trail** and a great view of
Kilauea Crater. Then walk to the floor of the crater and
the vent of the 1959 lava fountain. The trail passes over a
mile of steaming, still-cooling lava. On the east side of the
crater, the trail switchbacks through giant ferns to the
parking lot at the **Thurston Lava Tube**.

THE BIG ISLAND: RETURN TO HILO

Chain of Craters Road runs from Volcano House around hairpin turns as it cuts through vast lava fields toward Puna District. The road is closed at the Puna Coast due to lava flows blocking the most direct route to Highways 130 and 137. So drive to Keaau and then to the Puna Coast through Pahoa. From Cape Kumukahi, Route 132 branches west to Route 130 past Lava Tree State Monument to Pahoa, where a raised wooden sidewalk passes false-front fruit and vegetable stands. Visit the world's largest macadamia nut processor. Then return to Hilo's General Lyman Airport to turn in your car and take the evening flight to Kauai's Lihue Airport.

Suggested Schedule

8:00 a.m.	Breakfast and departure for Puna District on the Chain of Craters Road.
9:00 a.m.	Visit the Pu'u Loa Petroglyphs.
10:30 a.m.	Drive to Keaau on Highway 11.
12:00 noon	Lunch in Pahoa.
1:30 p.m.	Take Route 132 to Lava Tree State Park.
2:30 p.m.	Visit Cape Kumukahi Lighthouse.
4:00 p.m.	Visit the Mauna Loa Macadamia Nut Orchards and Mill in Keaau.
5:30 p.m.	Return to Hilo for departure to Kauai. Drop off car at the airport or in town.
6:30 p.m.	Flight to Lihue Airport, Kauai.
7:55 p.m.	Arrive in Lihue and pick up your rental car at the airport.
8:30 p.m.	Check into your Lihue or Wailua-Kapaa accommodations and enjoy a late dinner.

Orientation
About one-third of Volcanoes National Park is located in the Puna District, since 1983 covered with lava from Pu'u O'o and Kupaianaha vents and, recently, from the

Kupaianaha vent and lava pond, covering tens of thousands of acres up to 40 feet deep, flowing down from the 2,300-foot level to the sea at Kalapana through lava tubes. Route 130 through Kalapana is no longer passable. Visitors to this area have to come from the north through Pahoa on 130, returning on Route 137. The way to do this today is to head down Chain of Craters Road as far as you can go and then backtrack to Highway 11 east to Keaau, with the Puna region an option worth planning to see. The order of Puna's sightseeing highlights below will vary depending on your Puna route.

Sightseeing Highlights
▲▲ **Chain of Craters Road**—As an alternative to dashing back to Hilo on Route 11, start at the Crater Rim Road and pass numerous volcanic craters and pull-offs. Each pull-off has a vista of the coast below. Near the coast and the junction with Route 130, a roadside marker indicates the old Puna-Ka'u Trail, a half-mile one way to the Pu'u Loa Petroglyphs. Now you have to return to Highway 11 because the road is blocked by lava flow.

▲▲ **The Pu'u Loa Petroglyphs**—The trail traverses smooth lava and then pahoehoe to a large area where a wooden walkway encircles mounds of lava. The lava is etched with petroglyphs, such as stick figures surrounded by holes in which generations of Hawaiian fathers placed their infants' umbilical cords as offerings to the gods to bless their children with long lives.

▲ **Harry K. Brown Beach Park**—Near Kalapana, this park contains the ruins of **Kekaloa Heiau**. Swimming in the ocean is dangerous, but the park has a saltwater swimming pool built in the sand dunes and a protected ocean pond.

▲▲ **Cape Kumukahi Lighthouse**—At the easternmost point of Hawaii, this lighthouse was saved when the 1960 lava flow parted around it, then closed again on the other side to flow into the sea. Local legend says that on the night of the eruption an old woman (Pele in disguise?) seeking food was turned away by the people of Kapoho

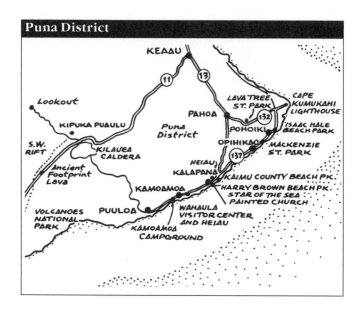

but welcomed by the lighthouse keeper. Yes, Kapoho was consumed by lava.

▲▲ **Lava Tree State Park**—This beautiful park holds a grove of ohia trees covered 12 feet deep in molten rock in 1790 to form a fossil forest. Huge fissures cracked open and, at the entrance to the park, huge trees have sent masses of tree roots into these cracks.

▲ **Keaau**—At the junction of Routes 130 and 11, this is the home of the **Mauna Loa Macadamia Nut Orchards and Mill**, the world's largest producer and processor of macadamia nuts. Enjoy free samples, watch mill operations, or buy gift boxes before heading for Hilo.

Getting to Kauai

Hawaiian Airlines has a one-stop (Honolulu) flight leaving Hilo for Lihue Airport, Kauai, at 6:30 p.m., and arriving on Kauai at 7:55 p.m., as well as a 5 p.m. flight arriving on Kauai at 6:25 p.m. Aloha Airlines has flights at 5:15 p.m., 6:15 p.m., and 6:40 p.m., with one and two stops and changes of planes, with these flights taking close to 2 hours.

Getting around Kauai

Across the street from the terminal at Lihue Airport is a string of car rental booths including: Alamo Rent-A-Car, 245-8953; American International Rent-A-Car, 245-9541; Avis Rent-A-Car, 245-3512; Budget Rent-A-Car, 245-4021; Dollar Rent-A-Car, 245-4708; Hertz, 245-3356; National Rent-A-Car, 245-3502; Robert's Hawaii Rent-A-Car, 245-4008; and United Rental, 245-8894. Cheaper deals may be had at Thrifty Rent-A-Car, 245-7388; Tropical Rent-A-Car, 245-6988; Wiki Wiki Wheels, 245-6944; and Rent-A-Wreck, 245-4755. Car rentals with a flat rate start at $21.95 a day, unlimited mileage. Rent-A-Wreck, Rent-A-Jeep Kauai, 245-9622, and Beach Boy, 245-2913 in Lihue and Westside, 332-8644 in Kalaheo, have car rentals at $16.95 or lower but may tack on a mileage charge. You won't need a four-wheel drive on Kauai.

Biking around Kauai is easy except for Kokee, the narrow shoulders on the roads, and increasingly heavy traffic. Cycling on Highways 50 and 56 (the Belt Road) is downright hazardous. Rental shops are: Bicycles Kauai, 1379 Kuhio Highway, in Kapaa, 822-3315, Aquatics Kauai, Kapaa, 822-9213; Peddle & Paddle, Hanalei, 826-9069; and South Shore Activities, next to the Sheraton in Poipu, 742-6873. Rentals cost $4 per hour or $12 to $20 per day or $100 per week.

Where to Stay

The least expensive, simplest down-to-earth hotels, motels, and apartments, mostly family-run, are in Lihue, Kauai's biggest town and the seat of government. Budget accommodations are even more plentiful here than in Hilo, with lots of small, basic, quiet, clean rooms with ceiling fans but no telephones or TVs. Rates are as low as $15 to $24 for single and double rooms. The best budget deals in Lihue with kitchenettes or kitchens are at **Hale Lihue Hotel**, 2931 Kalena Street off Rice, 245-3151, a pink, 2-story, very basic budget "motel" with 22 one-bedrooms for $25. Other budget choices are **Hale Pume-**

hana Motel, at 3083 Akahi Street, which has 17 units at
$22 to $30 for a 1-bedroom and a refrigerator, across
from the Lihue Shopping Center, Box 1828, 245-2106;
and **Ocean View Motel**, on the corner of Rice Street and
Wilcox Road, 3445 Wilcox Road, Nawiliwili, 245-6345,
pink again, seedy-looking outside, but spotless inside,
$25 for two.

The best moderate-priced choices in Wailua close to
the beach are: the **Kauai Sands Hotel**, 420 Papaloa
Road, 800-367-7000, 822-4951, next to the Coconut
Plantation Marketplace (Lihue side), 201 recently renovated rooms, $60 for single or double standard rooms or
a special package of $77 to $97 for two with a budget car
and unlimited mileage. Right on the beach near the Coconut Plantation is the **Kapaa Sands**, 380 Papaloa Road,
822-4901, 800-222-4901, a condo with $69 to $79 studios with kitchens, 3-night minimum in summer, 7 days
in winter, at $70. The **Kauai Beach Boy**, 822-3441 or
800-227-4700, on Waipouli Beach, offers a studio at $70.
The off-season price for an oceanfront studio apartment
at the **Mokihana of Kauai**, 796 Kuhio Highway,
822-3971, is $60 per night for a single or double room.
The oceanfront 2-bedroom duplexes are $80. Farther up
Highway 96 in Kapaa, the **Hotel Coral Reef**, 1516 Kuhio
Highway, 800-843-4569, is also on the ocean with its
own beach, close to a good swimming beach and restaurants. Comfortable but spare 1-bedrooms in the old wing
are $35 to $50, and upper rooms in the new wing with
ocean views start at $69 single or double.

The **Coco Palms Resort Hotel**, 800-542-2626 or
822-4921, was one of the first hotels built on the island.
With 35 acres of coconut trees and a nightly torch-
lighting ceremony, it's a popular tourist destination. The
coconut grove gardens and lagoon together with the
Polynesian and longhouse decor of the lobby and restaurants give the Coco Palms a distinctive and memorable
atmosphere among the island's hotels. Rates start at $110
per night. For $80 to $130, including a car rental, you can

get an ocean view 1-bedroom at the nearby **Aston Kauai Resort Hotel**, 800-272-5275, above Lydgate Park, with cascading pools, carp pond, and a huge longhouse-style lobby.

Where to Eat
Some of the best budget eating places in Lihue are in and around the Lihue Shopping Center. Big breakfasts for under $2 or Hawaiian dinners, like kalua pork with two eggs and lomi salmon, for under $3, at **Ma's Family**, 4277 Halenani Street at the corner of Kress, 245-3142, will spoil you for the rest of the trip. Saimin, with noodles, slivers of meat and fish, vegetables, wonton, and eggs in a delicious broth, costs less than $3 at **Hamamura Saimin Stand**, 2956 Kress Street, 245-3271, around the corner from Ma's.

Two restaurants in the Haleko Shops, across from the Lihue Shopping Center, will take care of those looking for big breakfasts, meat dinners, and Italian food: omelettes at **Eggberts**, 245-6325; and manicotti or cannelloni at **Casa Italiana**, 245-9586. After serving steak in garlic and wine sauce for 20 years in Lihue, the Slavonik steak special at **J. J. Broiler**, 246-4422, moved to the Anchor Cove Shopping Center. The restaurant now occupies two floors overlooking Kalapahi Beach next to the mammoth new Westin Kauai.

In Kapaa, **Al & Dons**, 822-4221, in the Kauai Sands Hotel, south of the Plantation Marketplace in Coconut Plantation, is one of the better restaurant deals, especially for breakfast. For a fresh fish dinner (or buffalo meat) at a moderate price, try the **Ono Family Restaurant**, 4-1292 Kuhio Highway, 822-1710, in the center of Kapaa, or the **Kapaa Fish & Chowder House**, 1639 Kuhio Highway, 822-7488, not far from the Hotel Coral Reef. The **Kountry Kitchen**, 1485 Kuhio Highway, 822-3511, serves hefty breakfasts. For Hawaiian food (laulau, lomi salmon, kalua pig) at reasonable prices, visit the **Aloha Diner** in the Waipouli complex, 4-971 Kuhio Highway, 822-3851.

Nightlife

The place to go in Lihue for disco and live music Wednesday through Saturday after 10 p.m. is the **Club Jetty Restaurant**, 245-4970 in Nawiliwili. Or, your excuse for visiting the **Westin Kauai Hotel** in Nawiliwili could be dancing at **The Paddling Club**, a 3-level disco. In Kapaa and Wailua, if you have the energy you can dance until 4 a.m. at the **Vanishing Point's** disco in Waipouli Plaza or to live music at the **Kauai Beach Boy's Boogie Palace**. Time for another or one last luau? Try the **Sheraton Coconut Beach**, 822-3455, or the **Aston Kauai Resort Hotel**, 245-3931, for live entertainment a few nights a week.

Itinerary Options

Kauai Canoe Expeditions, 245-5122, at the Kauai Canoe Club, near the **Menehune Fishpond** in Nawiliwili, and **Island Adventures**, Nawiliwili, 245-9662, will take you canoeing for 2 ½ hours up the **Huleia River** and along the fishpond into a wildfowl refuge. **Kauai by Kayak**, 245-9662, offers the same trip. **Kauai River Expeditions**, 826-9608, instructs you in the use of a combined canoe and kayak called a royak, then leads you up the **Kalihi Wai River**.

KAUAI: WAIMEA CANYON

Kauai may have been the first island visited by predecessors of the Polynesians, the legendary Menehune pygmies —strong, industrious, and skilled in stone-cutting. It is said that they built their dams, ditches, walls, and trails around Waimea (and Lihue) at night to avoid detection.

Waimea Canyon and Kokee State Park, leading to lookouts and trails on the Na Pali Coast, are among Hawaii's great scenic wonders.

Hiking trails lace Kokee State Park, and a short drive reveals one of the Hawaiian Islands' most spectacular views from the Kalalau Valley Lookout into Waimea Canyon and the Alakai Jungle.

Suggested Schedule

7:00 a.m.	Set out for Waimea Canyon after an early breakfast in Kapaa.
9:30 a.m.	Olu Pua Gardens.
11:00 a.m.	Hanapepe.
11:15 a.m.	Waimea.
11:45 a.m.	Waimea Canyon Road.
12:00 noon	Waimea Canyon Lookout.
12:30 p.m.	Puu Hinahina Lookout.
1:00 p.m.	Lunch at Kokee Lodge Restaurant.
1:45 p.m.	Kokee Natural History Museum.
2:15 p.m.	Drive to Kalalau Lookout.
3:00 p.m.	Drive to Makaha Ridge.
4:00 p.m.	Iliau Nature Loop Trail for sunset views.
5:00 p.m.	Return to Highway 50 on Kokee Road and east on Highway 50.
5:30 p.m.	Dinner in Hanapepe at the Green Garden.
7:00 p.m.	Check into your Poipu accommodations.
8:00 p.m.	Enjoy the nightlife along Poipu Beach.

Sightseeing Highlights

▲▲ **Ka'lmi Na'auao Hawai'i Nei,** formerly Olu Pua Botanical Gardens, now houses a school of hula and Hawaiian culture. The 12-acre estate, with its magnificent

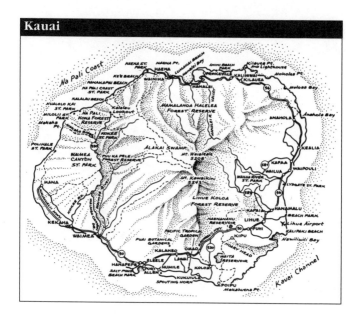

Kauai

gardens and tree groves, was originally built in the 1930s
for the Alexander family. Tours combine Hawaiian lore
and botanical information. Don't miss the Saturday Heri-
tage Garden Tour at 10 a.m. and 1 p.m., $15 per person
(332-7091 or 335-3628).

▲▲**Hanapepe**—This town is entered past Hanapepe
Canyon Lookout at the lush mouth of a green valley
planted in taro between red cliffs. The town's wooden
buildings hang over the west bank of the river. Besides
the canyon view, the best attractions in town are the
Green Garden Restaurant and several excellent art galleries. This former near "ghost town" is renewing rapidly
and will be one of the most interesting tiny towns on
Kauai.

▲▲**Waimea**—This town is full of history: missionary
and English, American and Russian settlements and
churches; the oldest house on the island (Gulick-Rowell
House); star-shaped Fort Elizabeth (not much left to see,
unfortunately); and, across the river, Captain Cook's 1778
landing site.

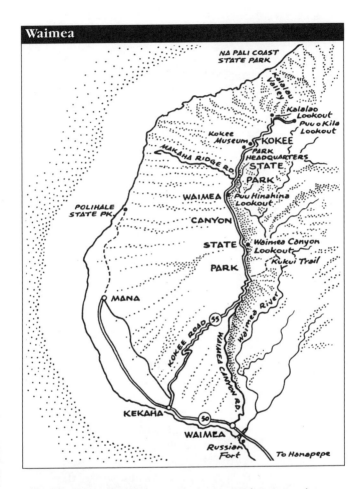

▲▲▲Waimea Canyon—The canyon is best seen in
early morning light, so beat the tour buses to the three
viewing platforms. The 3,000-foot gorge cuts a jagged
swath of mossy greens and blues into the reddish brown
volcanic walls of the Kokee Plateau. Easily accessible
trails in the Waimea Canyon State Park include the half-
mile round-trip **Iliau Nature Loop** (halfway between
the 8- and 9-mile markers), offering excellent views of
the canyon and Waialae Falls on the other side, and the
strenuous 3-mile **Kukui Trail** switchbacking down the
west canyon wall to the river below. Your best views,

however, will be above Kokee Camps at **Puu Ka Pele
Lookout** at the top of the gorge. Watch the jagged shapes
of the gorge change color with the sun. Pick up a **Kokee
Trails** map at the ranger station or (more likely) the
Kokee Natural History Museum, where you can book for
the Kokee Lodge and have lunch. **Kauai Mountain
Tours**, 742-7548 or 800-443-9180, has four-wheel-drive
tours to Kokee State Park and around Waimea Canyon.
▲▲▲ **Kokee State Park**—This park covers 4,345 acres
at 3,600 feet with 45 miles of hiking trails. The **Kokee
Natural History Museum** displays the park's flora and
fauna. It is open from 10 a.m. to 4 p.m. A lush meadow
set in a densely forested area is a good spot for a picnic.
The view is stunning from the lookout over **Kalalau Valley**, with waterfalls and vegetation cascading 4,000 feet
down the deepest valley on the Na Pali Coast. Drive
about a mile above the **Kalalau Lookout** to the **Puu
O'Kila Lookout** for another spectacular view of the Na
Pali Cliffs.

Where to Stay
Kokee Lodge's dozen cabins are furnished with everything you need for a stay of up to 5 days. Four newer
2-bedroom cedar cabins sleeping up to six rent for $45.
Four duplex units containing large studios rent for $35;
two other 2-bedrooms and two small studios also rent
for $35. ($25 cabins are a thing of the past, but these
cabins still are one of the best deals in Hawaii.) Definitely
reserve ahead: P.O. Box 819, Waimea, HI 96796, 335-6061.
   Next to Kahili Mountain Park (see Itinerary Options), a
few steps from a good snorkeling beach and the Beach
House Restaurant, Den and Dee Wilson's **Prince Kuhio
Condominiums** are one of the best hotel or condo deals
in Poipu. Their $54 (to $79) double rooms become a
$276 weekly rate for a very nicely furnished apartment
overlooking Prince Kuhio Park or gardens on the
grounds. Prices are higher December 15 to April 15, as is
true everywhere on Kauai except at the Kauai YMCA's
Camp Naue in Haena and the YWCA's **Camp Sloggett**
in Kokee with beautiful hiking trails all around. Purchase

a $10 membership card and for $10 per night you get a
mattress, space in the dormitory, kitchen and shower
facilities. Write: YMCA, 3094 Elua, Lihue, HI 96766,
245-5959; YWCA, P.O. Box 1786, Lihue, HI 96766,
246-9090.

Kapeana Center (Kapaa, 822-7968) is difficult to find,
secluded, with gorgeous views and wonderful rooms and
common spaces, indoors and out ($55-$65).

Near Spouting Horn, facing the surf and rocky coastline, **Gloria's Spouting Horn Bed & Breakfast**, 4464
Lawai Beach Road, Koloa, Kauai, HI 96756, 742-6995,
offers charming accommodations, mostly with ocean
views, tasty and ample breakfasts, and very reasonable
rates for Poipu at $50 to $90.

Eve Warner and Al Davis, who operate **Hawaii Bed &
Breakfast Service**, have built their own rental units
behind their house near Poipu Beach Park. **Poipu Plantation** has four 1-bedroom self-contained units, $65 to
$70 for a garden view and $70 to $75 for an ocean view,
and will soon have 2-bedroom units, $80 for ocean view,
and more 1-bedroom units, without breakfast. With a
lovely garden, great location, and perfect hosts, you can't
go wrong. Write Poipu Plantation, Route 1, Box 119,
Koloa, HI 96756, 742-7038 or 822-7771. The **Garden
Isle Cottages**, on Hoona Road to your left as you head
for Spouting Horn, offer a few of the least expensive local
accommodations. Artists Sharon and Robert Flynn have a
very comfortable and nicely decorated group of cottages
in a garden setting and others scattered around the
nearby area, $46 to $55 for a studio and $75 to $115 for a
double for two persons. Write Garden Isle Cottages,
R.R. 1, Box 355, Koloa, HI 96756, 742-6717. A very special treat at a moderate price is Hans and Sylvia Zeevat's
Koloa Landing Cottages, with nicely designed, furnished, equipped, and cared for 2-bedroom cottages
(only 2) at $75 single or double, and studios at $50 single
or double. Write Dolphin Realty, R.R. 1, Box 70, 2827
Poipu Road, Koloa, Kauai, HI 96756, 742-1470.

The Koloa area has some of the more unusual bed and
breakfast and alternative accommodations on Kauai,

away from the bustle of tourist activities but close to
Koloa and Poipu Beach. Rustic **Kahili Mountain Park**,
P.O. Box 298, Koloa, Kauai, HI 96756, 742-9921, operated
by the Seventh Day Adventist Church, is located seven
miles from Poipu Beach. Cabinettes with hot plates rent
for $20 double and cabins with a two-burner stove and
sink rent for $35. Overlooking Waita Reservoir, Vladimir
and Karna Knudsen's **Halemanu Guest Ranch** also is
rustic but very comfortable and homey, with cottages for
$75, and a cabin for $40, breakfast included.

Where to Eat

In Hanapepe, the **Green Garden**, 335-5422, is a top restaurant choice for good and plentiful Hawaiian, Oriental,
and American dishes such as barbecued chicken, tempura aki, breaded mahimahi, and incomparable home-
baked pies. Plants are everywhere, the screened wall
faces a garden, and you'll feel right at home. Get there
before 8:30 p.m. (closed on Tuesdays). On the right-hand
side of the street, before you come to the Green Garden,
is a huge dining room that looks like a local fraternal
club's banquet hall.

At the **Koloa Broiler**, 742-9122, on Koloa Road, you
order beef or mahimahi, cook it yourself on a central
broiler, toast some fresh baked bread, and help yourself
to the salad bar. For breakfast or lunch, definitely stop at
the **Garden Isle Bake Shoppe** (6:30 a.m.-9:00 p.m.) in
Kiahuna Shopping Village on Poipu Road, 742-6070.

The **Beach House**, 742-7575, rebuilt after Hurricane
Iwa, has a beautiful setting on Spouting Horn Road but is
the place to skip dinner and just have a Malihini Pupu
Platter and drinks. The **Plantation Gardens Restaurant**, 742-1695, at the Kiahuna Plantation Resort, is one
of the prettiest restaurants in the area, though you'll pay
$20 to $30 per person for dinner, atmosphere, decor,
crystal and silver, and the right wine. My favorite restaurant
on Kauai for a splurge lunch is **Gaylord's** in the courtyard of Kilohana near Puhi (Kaumualii Highway). The setting and the service match the delicious food. Reservations are advisable: 245-9593.

The **Kokee Lodge restaurant**, adjoining the gift shop, offers simple, basic, tasty snacks and dinners at moderate prices. After a few hours of walking or hiking, the food tastes very good.

Itinerary Options

Polihale State Park, down 4 miles of dirt cane road at the end of the extension of Highway 50 past Kekaha and Mana, has a fine white sand beach (swimming is dangerous). View the rugged Na Pali Cliffs and stay at a campground with a state park permit. The cliffs meet the sea at the remains of Polihale Heiau, where the souls of the dead made their last leap into the beyond. For swimming, the miles of white sand along **Kekaha State Park** are much safer. Great sunsets, too.

The **Na Pali Coast** can be seen by foot, boat, or helicopter. By foot, hike the 11-mile Kalalau Trail (pp. 159-160). By boat: **Captain Zodiac Raft Expeditions**, 800-422-7824, which costs $95 for a full day trip or $75 for a morning or afternoon excursion; and **Blue Odyssey Adventures**, 826-9033. The boat tours provide morning, afternoon, and full-day excursions from Hanalei for $75 to $125. Zodiac boats are very tough motorized rubber rafts that are unsinkably safe. **Lady Ann Charters**, 245-8538, and **Whitey's Na Pali Cruises**, 926-9221, offer cruiser trips with snorkeling along the Na Pali Coast; also from Hanalei Bay. **Na Pali Zodiac helicopter trips**, 826-9371 or 800-422-7824, are a thrilling (though expensive) way to see the Waimea Canyon and Na Pali Coast, especially early morning and sunset flights. The cost is from $100 to $200. Other reliable helicopter operations include **Papillon Helicopters**, 826-6591; **Jack Harter Helicopters**, 245-3774; or **Will Squire's Helicopter**, 245-7541. Kayak along the Na Pali Coast for a whole day (with lunch on an isolated beach) on a guided "trek" with **Kayak Kauai** for $95, call 742-7548 or 800-443-9180.

Golfers: Kukui-O-Lono Park just south of Kalaheo on Highway 50 is an excellent 9-hole golf course with only a $5 green fee and marvelous views down the south coast from high greens.

KAUAI: POIPU'S BEACHES

Enjoy fantasylike white sand beaches at Poipu Beach Park and, for the adventuresome, Shipwreck Beach and secluded beaches such as Mahaulepu. In the early afternoon, visit the Spouting Horn, stroll in Plantation Gardens, and browse in Kiahuna and Koloa.

Suggested Schedule

8:00 a.m.	Breakfast in Koloa Town and pack a beach picnic at the Big Save Market.
9:00 a.m.	A morning at Poipu Beach or Shipwreck and Mahaulepu beaches.
12:00 noon	Picnic lunch at the beach.
1:30 p.m.	Return to Poipu, clean up, and head for Spouting Horn.
2:30 p.m.	Visit Kiahuna Gardens and Kiahuna Shopping Village.
4:00 p.m.	Back to Koloa Town for sightseeing and browsing (possibly staying in town for an early dinner).
5:00 p.m.	Sunset at the beach, Koloa Landing, or happy hour somewhere comfortable.
6:00 p.m.	Dinner and overnight in Poipu.

Sightseeing Highlights

▲▲ **Koloa**—A plantation town that developed in the mid-1800s around a sugar mill, Koloa declined with the demise of the sugar industry until tourism in the early 1970s started the restoration of "Old Koloa Town." Just a few miles from the Poipu Beach resort hotels and condos, Koloa's shops and restaurants, catering mainly to tourists, continue to grow.

▲▲ **Poipu**—Kauai's south side is the center of tourist activity on Kauai. In November 1982, Hurricane Iwa hit Poipu with devastating force. Poipu recovered completely and thrives today as though nothing happened or ever will again. The center of the area is Poipu Beach

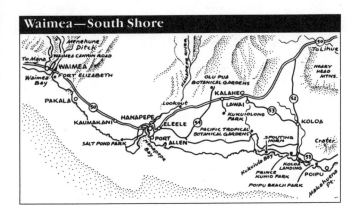

Park, with one of the best swimming beaches on the
island. There's great snorkeling and bodysurfing around
the beach. Walk along the beaches in front of the hotels
and condos to the west, from the Waiohai Resort to the
Sheraton Kauai.

▲**Spouting Horn**—A lava tube that extends into the sea
with its mouth on the rocky shore gushing spumes from
wave action high in the air, depending on surf conditions.
Reached by Lawai Road off Poipu Road, the Kuku'ula Bay
area, birthplace of Prince Kuhio, is quite beautiful. At the
far end of the large parking area for Spouting Horn is the
best place in Hawaii to buy shell jewelry, a daily flea market run by the jewelry makers. It's full of bargains.

▲▲**Shipwreck Beach**—This beach along the coast east
of Poipu is Kauai as it used to be decades ago. A broad,
sandy, rock-strewn beach extending for about a mile
along a reef-protected shoreline, Shipwreck is reached
via the canefield road that extends from Poipu Road past
the Poipu Kai Resort and now the new luxurious Hyatt
Regency. If you're walking, head out there in the morning
before the hottest sun hits the canefields. On the east end
of Shipwreck is an ironwood grove and beyond that is
Kawelikoa Point, which overlooks the beach and rocky
coastline to the east, ideal for camping. Narrow tracks
along the edges of the canefield meander along the
shoreline for several miles to Molehu Point and Kuahona

Point. The direct route to **Mahaulepu Beach** follows the
main cane road for about two miles, curving toward Hoary
Head Ridge, to a crossroads with another main cane
road (with a line of telephone poles). Turn right, past a
quarry to the right, until you see a road on your right
leading to the beach. Farther to the east is the even
more remote **Hidden Valley Beach**. For a great camping
vacation within walking distance of Poipu, these beaches
and coves are rare finds. Just leave them as you find them.
One easy and fun way to find out where all of these
beaches are located is to call **CJM Country Stables**,
245-6666, located near Mahaulepu Beach, and arrange
for a horseback riding tour through the whole area; an
hour along the ocean, $25 (10 a.m. and 12:30 p.m.); 3
hours including breakfast, $55 (starting at 8:30 a.m.); or 2
hours for $44.

Itinerary Options
▲▲▲ **National Tropical Botanical Garden**, located on
Hailima Road about two miles south of Lawai, this is the
only tropical research garden in the United States, with a
staggering abundance of tropical flora in its collection,
adding about a thousand plants each year. A 2-hour
guided tour of the 186-acre site, only given on Tuesday
and Thursday mornings at 9 a.m., costs $15 per person
and requires advance reservations. (Write to Box 340,
Lawai, Kauai, HI 96765; tel. 332-7361.) The tour includes
the estate started by Queen Emma, wife of Kamehameha
IV, in the 1870s, and developed by the Allerton family.
   Diving and snorkeling: Fathom Five Divers, Poipu
Road, Poipu, 742-6991, rents snorkeling and diving
equipment and offers instruction and tours in scuba div-
ing. Also try **Aquatics Kauai**, 822-9213, and **Sea Sage
Dive Center**, 822-3841. Rent surfboards at **Progressive
Expressions**, Old Koloa Town, 742-6041, or **Waiohai
Beach Services**, Waiohai Resort, Poipu, 742-7051.

KAUAI: NORTH SHORE AND HANALEI VALLEY

Hanalei is about 50 miles from Poipu. The ambitious goal of today's drive is to see as many beach gems between Kapaa and Haena as possible without the benefit of wings, and especially to soak in the scenic nine miles between Hanalei and Haena.

Suggested Schedule

7:00 a.m.	Early breakfast and checkout.
8:00 a.m.	Stop at Kealia, Anahola, and Moloaa beaches.
10:00 a.m.	Kong Lung Center, Lighthouse Road.
10:30 a.m.	Mokolea Point's Crater Hill, the Kilauea Lighthouse and Bird Sanctuary or both.
12:00 noon	Option: Picnic lunch at Secret Beach or Anini Beach.
2:00 p.m.	Hanalei Valley Lookout for a panoramic view of the river, the valley, and its taro fields against the background of the Na Pali Coast Range.
2:15 p.m.	Hanalei Town and Hanalei Beach.
2:45 p.m.	View of Lumahai Beach and Haena Beach Park en route to Kee Beach.
3:15 p.m.	Kee Beach.
4:30 p.m.	Return to Hanalei Town for sunset from the Hanalei pier over Hanalei Bay.
7:00 p.m.	Dinner in Hanalei and evening at the Tahiti Nui or back in Poipu.

Sightseeing Highlights

▲▲ **Kealia Beach**—This is the first in a string of beautiful white sand beaches north of Kapaa. From here take the scenic old coastal road almost to Anahola Bay where it returns to Highway 56.

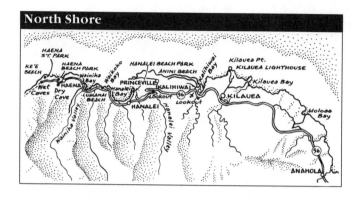

North Shore

▲▲**Anahola Bay Beach Park**—Just a few miles north of Kapaa, this beach is lovely for relaxation and picnics but hazardous for swimming.

▲▲**Moloaa Beach**—This beach is reached off the Koolau Road. Take a right turn off Highway 56 at the Papaya Plantation and Information Center. From Moloaa Bay take a right turn on Koolau Road to return to Highway 56.

▲▲**Larson's Beach**—A lovely narrow stretch of secluded sand, this beach is found (with difficulty) down the same Koolau Road, which you take for another mile past the turnoff to Moloaa Beach. Take a cane road to the right, then switch left for a mile onto a dirt road lined on both sides with barbed wire. Pass through a gate and travel another half-mile of dirt road until you reach the beach.

▲▲**Mokolea Point's Crater Hill**—Located on a direct road to the right off Kilauea Road, this point has a splendid panoramic view of the coast and surrounding countryside from a 560-foot viewpoint straight down to the turquoise sea pounding on the jagged, curved lava cliffs. You might see a great frigate bird, with its 8-foot wingspan, riding air currents.

▲▲**The Kilauea Lighthouse and Bird Sanctuary**—Drive straight down Kilauea Road to the lighthouse with the largest "clamshell lens" in the world. It sends its bea-

con 90 miles out to sea. Permanent and migratory birds
fill the peninsula, including the red-footed booby, the
white-tailed and red-tailed tropic bird, the Laysan
albatross, and the wedge-tailed shearwater. A small
museum at the lighthouse has pictures of all the birds.
The craggy point is under the protection of the U.S. Fish
and Wildlife Service. You can borrow binoculars to look
for green sea turtles, spinner dolphins, or whales in season. The Kilauea Point Refuge is open daily except Saturday from noon to 4 p.m. A $2 fee for each adult.

▲**Kong Lung Store**—Located in the Kong Lung Center
in Old Kilauea Town, on the way to the lighthouse, this is
Kauai's oldest plantation general store (1881). In addition
to everything you would expect to find in a country
general store, one room contains an art gallery with very
high quality carvings, pottery, and other Pacific area
items. Before leaving Kilauea, pick up some delicious
bread or pastries at **The Bread Also Rises** in the Kong
Lung Center, and the rest of picnic fare, which is even
better than the famous **Jacques Bakery** around the corner on Oka Street.

▲**Sylvester's Catholic Church**—This church is
located just before the turn onto Kilauea Road to the
lighthouse. It has an octagonal design made out of lava
and native wood with interior murals of the stations of
the cross painted by Jean Charlot, a well-known island
artist. The church also is the starting point for a short
walk to the Slippery Slide, which, to avoid injury and
needless drenching, will be overlooked here.

▲▲**Secret Beach** (or Kauapea Beach)—One of the most
beautiful, longest, and widest beaches in Hawaii. Turn
left on Kauapea Road (.8 mile from Kong Lung). Watch on
your right for a fence (with a marine reserve notice on it)
and a dirt path down a long steep trail through beautiful
tropical growth to the beach. Beautifully calm in summer,
the waves get wicked in winter. As a secluded camping
spot, and a favorite nude beach, it's hard to beat.

▲▲**Kalihiwai Beach**—Just past Kilauea down the first

Kalihiwai Road, you'll come to a dead end at a white sand beach lined by ironwoods which is perfect for sheltered camping. Swimming and bodysurfing are ideal in summer months. Swimming is safe in the lagoon where the river meets the ocean. The quiet little village on Kalihiwai Bay was destroyed by tidal waves in 1946 and 1957. You can walk along the beach from Secret Beach to Kalihiwai.

▲▲ **Anini Beach**—Just before you reach Princeville on the second Kalihiwai Road, this beach is about a mile past the first one to the right just past the Kalihiwai Lookout and Princeville Airport. Turn on Anini Road to miles of white sand beach that is sheltered by the longest exposed reef off Kauai. This beach is great for windsurfing year-round and for summer swimming and snorkeling in the shallow water. Camping at the south end of the beach, with facilities, requires a county permit.

▲ **Princeville**—Continuing to grow in thousand-acre hunks over a gorgeous rolling plateau overlooking Hanalei Bay, this area has the largest concentration of the good life in the Hawaiian Islands in a mixture of single-family homes, condominiums, and the Sheraton Princeville Hotel. The 27-hole golf course has a greens fee of $40, plus $26 for a mandatory golf cart, for an exquisite round of golf.

▲▲ **The Hanalei Valley Lookout**—Just past the entrance to Princeville, pull off to the left to view a patchwork of ancient taro fields that carpet the valley below. The Hanalei River is a silver loop as it flows placidly to Hanalei Bay, in turn cradled by a 3,500-foot protective pali. Over 900 acres of Hanalei Valley comprise the **Hanalei National Wildlife Refuge**, so you can drive down **Hanalei Valley Road** but can't get out of your car except at the restored **Haraguchi Rice Mill** or at the end of the road.

▲▲ **Hanalei Town**—Featuring a beautiful bay for sailing and water sports, an ideal boat anchorage, and exceptional restaurants, this small town with a pleasant mixture of old and new is barely resisting the pressures of commercialization. New commercial construction along Highway 560, across from old Hanalei, obviously tries to be compatible with the local building style, but the newness seems out of place and period viewed in relation to the **Ching Young Store**, the **Hanalei Museum**, the **Waioli Mission House** and **Waioli Mission Hall**, and **Waioli Huila Church**.

▲▲ **Hanalei Beach**—A perfect wide curving crescent behind Hanalei Town, this beach is best for cautious swimming in summer.

▲▲ **Lumahai Beach**—This beach achieved instant and lasting fame in the movie *South Pacific* and is justifiably one of the most photographed beaches in the islands. Currents and riptides make swimming here very dangerous unless the water is extremely calm.

▲▲ **Haena Beach Park**—Just past Haena Point, the Bali Ha'i beach in *South Pacific*, is this beautiful white sand beach with coconut palms, lush foliage, and tall cliffs rising from the sea. With a camping permit, you can camp in this 5-acre park.

▲▲ **Kee Beach**—This is one of the most perfect beaches in Hawaii for picnicking, swimming, and snorkeling in summer and watching the high surf in winter months. Nearby are the remains of a heiau, the temple of the goddess of the hula where sacred dances were taught. Beyond are the cliffs of Na Pali and the beginning of the **Kalalau Trail**.

The trailhead to Kalalau Valley is opposite the Kee parking area and clearly marked. Walk about a half-mile up the trail and look back for a wonderful view of Kee Beach and the Na Pali Coast.

Beaches of Kauai

CAUTION! Starting at Nukolii Beach, north of Lihue, North Shore beaches can be extremely treacherous for swimmers. Wailua Beach is beautiful, but heavy surf causes a strong backwash. Kapaa Beach is all right at low tide, thanks to reef protection, especially north of the Waikaea Canal, but beware at high tide. The bays on either side of Anapalau Point, reached by the old coast road paralleling Kealia Beach, and Opana Beach north of Opana Point, have some of the island's best snorkeling, using appropriate caution. Rough waters, surface currents, and backwash make most of the North Shore beaches dangerous. This is true at Kealia Beach, Aliomanu Beach, Kukuna Beach, Moloaa Beach, Kaakaaniu Beach, Waipake Beach, and others to Kilauea Bay and Kilauea Point National Wildlife Refuge.

Near Princeville, there's no safe swimming until Hanalei Pier, and even there swimming can be unsafe due to rip currents in winter. Stay close to shore. Kahalahala and Lumahai beaches are as dangerous as they are beautiful, for gazing at but not for swimming. The same is true from Wainiha Beach, Wainiha Kuau Beach, Kaonihi and Kanaha beaches, to Makua Beach, where you can snorkel inside the reef. Both Haena Beach and Kee Beach are not for swimming. In other words, *don't swim outside protected areas on the North Shore.*

Where to Eat
Norberto's El Café 4-1373 Kuhio Highway, Kapaa, 822-3362, has opened an inexpensive and delicious restaurant in Hanalei. It doesn't look like much outside, but the food is great, including desserts that Mexican restaurants usually shun. Salads at **Charo's** in Haena, next to the Hanalei Colony Resort, are your best bet there. The **Shell House** at the intersection of Kuhio Highway and Aku Road (826-9301) serves three excellent meals a day. Like the **Tahiti Nui** down the street, the bar is open until 2 a.m. Eat family-style or enjoy one of the best luaus on the island (Monday, Wednesday, and Friday) at the **Tahiti Nui**, 826-9301. The atmosphere is the best part of this restaurant but the fish dinners are excellent.

Itinerary Options
The 11-mile **Kalalau Trail** along the massive, fluted cliffs of the Na Pali Coast from Kee Beach to Hanakapiai (don't miss **Hanakapiai Falls**), Hoolulu, Waiahuakua, Hanakoa

(swimming pool and falls), and Kalalau valleys is the best hike on the island and one of the best in Hawaii. One way takes about 8 hours. Take Highway 56 through Hanalei and Haena on the North Coast to Kee Beach. There's a parking lot at the end of Highway 56.

In summer be prepared to see some people hiking in the nude along these enchanting trails through Eden-like terrain, surrounded by thick ferns, mountain orchids, bamboo, bananas, monkeypod, guava, morning glories, kukui, koa, mango, and hala trees. You can eat delicious crisp mountain apples here. Don't venture on the trail to Hanakoa and beyond unless you're in excellent shape. There are some very narrow ledges past Hanakoa that look over sheer drops of over 1,000 feet! Consider just a one-day round-trip to Hanakoa Stream. Camp at Hanakapiai and not in mosquito-infested Hanakoa Valley. Bring lots of repellent.

For an unusual experience, try a double-hulled canoe sail on Hanalei Bay with **Ancient Hawaiian Adventures**, 826-6088.

In the Hanalei area, **Pooku Stables**, 826-6777, offers horse treks on the beach, to nearby waterfalls, and into the hills overlooking Hanalei Valley for wonderful views.

KAUAI: WAILUA RIVER STATE PARK AND LIHUE

The final day in Hawaii presents choices for different tastes: if you can tolerate quantities of tourists, Wailua River State Park, the former home of Hawaii's royalty midway along the east coast, is well worth the visit. On the outskirts of Lihue, two restored estates combine plantation history, a superb lunch, and unusual shopping. And in Lihue, whale-watching may be in season.

Kauai has direct flights to the West Coast, but excursion airfares may require that you return to the U.S. mainland through Honolulu. An inter-island flight in the late afternoon can be arranged to conveniently connect with a flight to the mainland.

Suggested Schedule

8:00 a.m.	Breakfast and checkout.
9:00 a.m.	Wailua River State Park or visit the Grove Farm Homestead.
12:00 noon	Leisurely lunch at Kilohana Plantation.
1:30 p.m.	Visit the Kilohana Plantation shops.
3:00 p.m.	Return rental car at the airport.
4:00 p.m.	Inter-island flight to Honolulu.
6:00 p.m.	Return flight to the mainland.

Sightseeing Highlights

The **Wailua River** is best known for the motorboat tours that leave every half hour from the marina for the 1½-hour trip to the **Fern Grotto**. The trip is beautiful and for $8 a good value, even if you have to endure the singing of Ke Kali Nei Au ("The Hawaiian Wedding Song") at the Grotto.

▲▲**The Grove Farm Homestead**—In Nawiliwili, about halfway up Nawiliwili Road (Highway 58), the farm was founded as a sugarcane plantation in 1864 by the son of a Hanalei missionary family. Today the main house, planta-

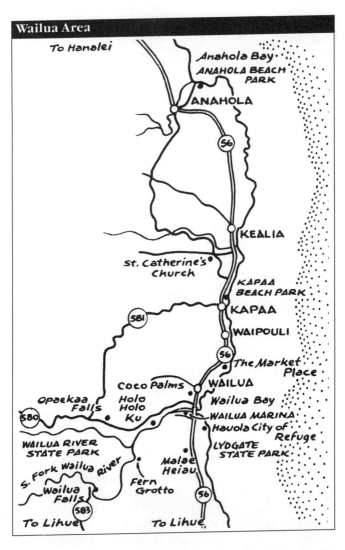

Wailua Area

To Hanalei

Anahola Bay
ANAHOLA BEACH PARK

ANAHOLA

56

KEALIA

St. Catherine's Church

KAPAA BEACH PARK

581

KAPAA

WAIPOULI

56

The Market Place

WAILUA

Coco Palms

Holo Holo Ku

Wailua Bay

Opaekaa Falls

WAILUA MARINA

580

Hauola City of Refuge

WAILUA RIVER STATE PARK

LYDGATE STATE PARK

S. Fork Wailua River

Malae Heiau

Fern Grotto

Wailua Falls

583

To Lihue

56

To Lihue

tion office, workers' cottages and outbuildings, orchards
and gardens are well preserved for tourists. Seeing the
homestead requires more preplanning than most other
attractions. Tours are provided only on Monday, Wednesday, and Thursday at 10 a.m. and 1:15 p.m. and last about

2 hours. The cost is about $5. Write to Grove Farm Homestead, P.O. Box 1631, Lihue, Kauai, HI 96766, or call 245-3202 at least a month in advance.

▲▲ **Kilohana Plantation**—With 35 acres of landscaped grounds, on Highway 50, 2 miles south of Lihue, this plantation was built in 1935 by George Wilcox, who also founded Grove Farm Plantation. It has been restored to its original condition and furnishings to combine a museum, a collection of unique boutiques and art galleries, and a marvelous restaurant.

▲ **Kalapaki Beach Park**—On Nawiliwili Bay, this park is a beautiful place to get just a few more minutes or hours on the beach before leaving for the mainland.

▲ **Kauai Museum**, 245-6931, on Rice Street, has a permanent natural history collection and changing Hawaiiana exhibits. The book and gift shop is a good place to pick up souvenirs of your trip. The museum is open Monday through Friday, from 9:30 a.m. to 4 p.m., and admission is $3 for adults, children free.

Where to Eat

Gaylord's, 245-9593, at Kilohana, might stretch the dwindling remainder of your budget for dinner, but for lunch it is reasonable. The setting and the food are special. As the last meal before heading to the mainland, to celebrate your 22-day journey, I can't think of a better place. Fish of the day, chicken, duck, or vegetarian dishes, pasta, or Gaylord's Papaya Runneth Over (stuffed with baby shrimp), with Chocolate Decadence Cake or other delicious desserts, make for a fitting feast. The **Hanamaulu Restaurant and Tea House**, 245-2511, 4 miles north on Highway 56, also serves a perfect farewell meal. The beautifully landscaped garden, complete with stone pagoda and a carp pond, is the setting for Chinese and Japanese plate lunches that compare with the best on the islands.

Itinerary Options

Wailua Falls, above Fern Grotto, is reached on Highway
583 from Highway 56, two miles north of Lihue. If there's
been heavy rain, you'll see twin falls tumbling over an
80-foot cliff. Fern Grotto is a cave (lava tube) draped with
ferns. It is beautiful but crowded, unless you take the first
20-minute boat ride from Wailua Marina in the morning.
Be prepared to be serenaded with "The Hawaiian Wed-
ding Song" as you float through the thick riverside
foliage. Contact **Smith Motor Boat Service**, 822-4111,
or **Waialeale Boat Tours**, 822-4908. The cost is $10 per
adult and $5 for children under 12.

Lydgate State Park at the mouth of the Wailua River
contains the remains of an ancient place of refuge for
Hawaiian kapu breakers. By the river there are ancient
petroglyphs in the rocks, part of the nearby heiau.

Holo-Holo-Ku Heiau, a mile up the north bank of
the river, was the temple to which royal mothers came to
ensure the royalty of their child by leaning against the
birthstone, which remains intact. The bellstone rang to
announce the birth of a royal Hawaiian. There is also a
sacrificial stone.

If you have extra time, from Highway 56 take Highway
580 for 6.6 miles to the trailhead of **Kuilai Ridge Trail**, a
2-hour hike past waterfalls and orchids to two spectacular coast viewpoints.

Lady Anne Cruises, 245-8538, has a 2½-hour whale-
watching cruise for $35, leaving Lihue at 9 a.m. with an
expert commentator from the Pacific Whale Foundation.

INDEX

Other Books from John Muir Publications

Adventure Vacations: From Trekking in New Guinea to Swimming in Siberia, Bangs 256 pp. $17.95

Asia Through the Back Door, 3rd ed., Steves and Gottberg 326 pp. $15.95

Buddhist America: Centers, Retreats, Practices, Morreale 400 pp. $12.95

Bus Touring: Charter Vacations, U.S.A., Warren with Bloch 168 pp. $9.95

California Public Gardens: A Visitor's Guide, Sigg 304 pp. $16.95

Catholic America: Self-Renewal Centers and Retreats, Christian-Meyer 325 pp. $13.95

Complete Guide to Bed & Breakfasts, Inns & Guesthouses, 1991-92, Lanier 520 pp. $16.95

Costa Rica: A Natural Destination, Sheck 280 pp. $15.95

Elderhostels: The Students' Choice, 2nd ed., Hyman 304 pp. $15.95

Environmental Vacations: Volunteer Projects to Save the Planet, Ocko 240 pp. $15.95

Europe 101: History & Art for the Traveler, 4th ed., Steves and Openshaw 372 pp. $15.95

Europe Through the Back Door, 9th ed., Steves 432 pp. $16.95

Floating Vacations: River, Lake, and Ocean Adventures, White 256 pp. $17.95

Gypsying After 40: A Guide to Adventure and Self-Discovery, Harris 264 pp. $14.95

The Heart of Jerusalem, Nellhaus 336 pp. $12.95

Indian America: A Traveler's Companion, Eagle/Walking Turtle 424 pp. $16.95 (2nd ed. available 7/91 $16.95)

Mona Winks: Self-Guided Tours of Europe's Top Museums, Steves and Openshaw 456 pp. $14.95

Opera! The Guide to Western Europe's Great Houses, Zietz 280 pp. $18.95

Paintbrushes and Pistols: How the Taos Artists Sold the West, Taggett and Schwarz 280 pp. $17.95

The People's Guide to Mexico, 8th ed., Franz 608 pp. $17.95

The People's Guide to RV Camping in Mexico, Franz with Rogers 320 pp. $13.95

Ranch Vacations: The Complete Guide to Guest and Resort, Fly-Fishing, and Cross-Country Skiing Ranches, 2nd ed., Kilgore 396 pp. $18.95

The Shopper's Guide to Art and Crafts in the Hawaiian Islands, Schuchter 272 pp. $13.95

The Shopper's Guide to Mexico, Rogers and Rosa 224 pp. $9.95

Ski Tech's Guide to Equipment, Skiwear, and Accessories, edited by Tanler 144 pp. $11.95

Ski Tech's Guide to Maintenance and Repair, edited by Tanler 160 pp. $11.95

A Traveler's Guide to Asian Culture, Chambers 224 pp. $13.95

Traveler's Guide to Healing Centers and Retreats in North America, Rudee and Blease 240 pp. $11.95

Understanding Europeans, Miller 272 pp. $14.95

Undiscovered Islands of the Caribbean, 2nd ed., Willes 232 pp. $14.95

Undiscovered Islands of the Mediterranean, Moyer and Willes 232 pp. $14.95

A Viewer's Guide to Art: A Glossary of Gods, People, and Creatures, Shaw and Warren 152 pp. $10.95

2 to 22 Days Series

These pocket-size itineraries (4½" × 8") are a refreshing departure from ordinary guidebooks. Each offers 22 flexible daily itineraries that can be used to get the most out of vacations of any length. Included are not only "must see" attractions but also little-known villages and hidden "jewels" as well as valuable general information.

22 Days Around the World, Rapoport and Willes 200 pp. $9.95 (1992 ed. available 8/91 $11.95)
2 to 22 Days Around the Great Lakes, 1991 ed., Schuchter 176 pp. $9.95
22 Days in Alaska, Lanier 128 pp. $7.95
22 Days in the American Southwest, 2nd ed., Harris 176 pp. $9.95
22 Days in Asia, Rapoport and Willes 136 pp. $7.95 (1992 ed. available 8/91 $9.95)
22 Days in Australia, 3rd ed., Gottberg 148 pp. $7.95 (1992 ed. available 8/91 $9.95)
22 Days in California, 2nd ed., Rapoport 176 pp. $9.95
22 Days in China, Duke and Victor 144 pp. $7.95
22 Days in Europe, 5th ed., Steves 192 pp. $9.95
22 Days in Florida, Harris 136 pp. $7.95 (1992 ed. available 8/91 $9.95)
2 to 22 Days in France, 1991 ed., Steves 192 pp. $9.95
22 Days in Germany, Austria & Switzerland, 3rd ed., Steves 136 pp. $7.95
2 to 22 Days in Great Britain, 1991 ed., Steves 192 pp. $9.95
22 Days in Hawaii, 2nd ed., Schuchter 144 pp. $7.95 (1992 ed. available 8/91 $9.95)
22 Days in India, Mathur 136 pp. $7.95
22 Days in Japan, Old 136 pp. $7.95
22 Days in Mexico, 2nd ed., Rogers and Rosa 128 pp. $7.95
2 to 22 Days in New England, 1991 ed., Wright 176 pp. $9.95
2 to 22 Days in New Zealand, 1991 ed., Schuchter 176 pp. $9.95
2 to 22 Days in Norway, Sweden, & Denmark, 1991 ed., Steves 184 pp. $9.95
2 to 22 Days in the Pacific Northwest, 1991 ed., Harris 184 pp. $9.95
22 Days in the Rockies, Rapoport 176 pp. $9.95
22 Days in Spain & Portugal, 3rd ed., Steves 136 pp. $7.95
22 Days in Texas, Harris 176 pp. $9.95
22 Days in Thailand, Richardson 176 pp. $9.95
22 Days in the West Indies, Morreale and Morreale 136 pp. $7.95

Parenting Series

Being a Father: Family, Work, and Self, *Mothering* Magazine 176 pp. $12.95
Preconception: A Woman's Guide to Preparing for Pregnancy and Parenthood, Aikey-Keller 232 pp. $14.95
Schooling at Home: Parents, Kids, and Learning, *Mothering* Magazine 264 pp. $14.95
Teens: A Fresh Look, *Mothering* Magazine 240 pp. $14.95

"Kidding Around" Travel Guides for Young Readers

Written for kids eight years of age and older. Generously illustrated in two colors with imaginative characters and images. An adventure to read and a treasure to keep.

Kidding Around Atlanta, Pedersen 64 pp. $9.95
Kidding Around Boston, Byers 64 pp. $9.95
Kidding Around Chicago, Davis 64 pp. $9.95
Kidding Around the Hawaiian Islands, Lovett 64 pp. $9.95
Kidding Around London, Lovett 64 pp. $9.95
Kidding Around Los Angeles, Cash 64 pp. $9.95
Kidding Around the National Parks of the Southwest, Lovett 108 pp. $12.95
Kidding Around New York City, Lovett 64 pp. $9.95
Kidding Around Paris, Clay 64 pp. $9.95
Kidding Around Philadelphia, Clay 64 pp. $9.95
Kidding Around San Francisco, Zibart 64 pp. $9.95
Kidding Around Santa Fe, York 64 pp. $9.95
Kidding Around Seattle, Steves 64 pp. $9.95
Kidding Around Washington, D.C., Pedersen 64 pp. $9.95

Environmental Books for Young Readers
Written for kids eight years and older. Examines the environmental issues and opportunities that today's kids will face during their lives.

The Indian Way: Learning to Communicate with Mother Earth, McLain 114 pp. $9.95

The Kids' Environment Book: What's Awry and Why, Pedersen 192 pp. $13.95

Rads, Ergs, and Cheeseburgers: The Kids' Guide to Energy and the Environment, Yanda 108 pp. $12.95

"Extremely Weird" Series for Young Readers
Written for kids eight years of age and older. Designed to help kids appreciate the world around them. Each book includes full-color photographs with detailed and entertaining descriptions.

Extremely Weird Bats, Lovett 48 pp. $9.95 paper

Extremely Weird Frogs, Lovett 48 pp. $9.95 paper

Extremely Weird Spiders, Lovett 48 pp. $9.95 paper

Automotive Repair Manuals
How to Keep Your VW Alive, 14th ed., 440 pp. $19.95

How to Keep Your Subaru Alive 480 pp. $19.95

How to Keep Your Toyota Pickup Alive 392 pp. $19.95

How to Keep Your Datsun/Nissan Alive 544 pp. $19.95

Other Automotive Books
The Greaseless Guide to Car Care Confidence: Take the Terror Out of Talking to Your Mechanic, Jackson 224 pp. $14.95

Off-Road Emergency Repair & Survival, Ristow 160 pp. $9.95

Ordering Information
If you cannot find our books in your local bookstore, you can order directly from us. Please check the "Available" date above. If you send us money for a book not yet available, we will hold your money until we can ship you the book. Your books will be sent to you via UPS (for U.S. destinations). UPS will not deliver to a P.O. Box; please give us a street address. Include $2.75 for the first item ordered and $.50 for each additional item to cover shipping and handling costs. For airmail within the U.S., enclose $4.00. All foreign orders will be shipped surface rate; please enclose $3.00 for the first item and $1.00 for each additional item. Please inquire about foreign airmail rates.

Method of Payment
Your order may be paid by check, money order, or credit card. We cannot be responsible for cash sent through the mail. All payments must be made in U.S. dollars drawn on a U.S. bank. Canadian postal money orders in U.S. dollars are acceptable. For VISA, MasterCard, or American Express orders, include your card number, expiration date, and your signature, or call (800) 888-7504. Books ordered on American Express cards can be shipped only to the billing address of the cardholder. Sorry, no C.O.D.'s. Residents of sunny New Mexico, add 5.875% tax to the total.

Address all orders and inquiries to:
John Muir Publications
P.O. Box 613
Santa Fe, NM 87504
(505) 982-4078
(800) 888-7504